MORE PRAISE FOR *THE SPACE BETWEEN*

'*The Space Between* is a riotous, side-splittingly funny tribute to the insanity of our twenties and the lessons we learn in the most unexpected of places. Above all, it is a tribute to joy, friendship and the brilliance of women – those we know, those we admire and those we are capable of finding within ourselves. I loved it.' – **Clementine Ford, bestselling author and host of *The Big Sister Hotline***

'*The Space Between* is a fantastic resource for young people – a book I needed in my twenties. Michelle and Zara are smart, funny, relatable and reliable, and are always committed to using their platform to support and amplify diverse women.' – **Carly Findlay, OAM, writer, speaker and appearance activist**

ABOUT THE AUTHORS

Michelle Andrews and **Zara McDonald** are Melbourne-based journalists and broadcasters, aged twenty-six. They met working as writers for Mamamia, and in March 2018 launched Australia's top pop culture podcast *Shameless*, 'for smart people who like dumb stuff.' As of May 2020, the podcast has been downloaded more than 10 million times. They now run Shameless Media, under which they have produced four separate podcasts that have each hit number one on the Australian Apple Podcast Charts.

The Space Betw een

**Chaos. Questions. Magic.
Welcome to your twenties.**

Michelle Andrews & Zara McDonald

PENGUIN
VIKING

VIKING

UK | USA | Canada | Ireland | Australia
India | New Zealand | South Africa | China

Viking is part of the Penguin Random House group of companies
whose addresses can be found at global.penguinrandomhouse.com

Penguin
Random House
Australia

First published by Viking in 2020

Cover and internal design by Alissa Dinallo
Internal illustrations by Sarah Firth
Typeset in 10.5/14 pt Mercury and 11/14 pt Brandon Grotesque by Post Pre-press Group, Brisbane

Printed and bound in Australia by Griffin Press, part of Ovato, an accredited
ISO AS/NZS 14001 Environmental Management Systems printer

  A catalogue record for this
book is available from the
National Library of Australia

ISBN 978 1 76089 461 0

penguin.com.au

MIX
Paper from
responsible sources
FSC® C009448

For anyone who saw a terribly designed pink-and-yellow podcast logo in their feed and decided, 'I'm going to give these girls a shot.'

Contents

PART 1:**LOVE**

PART 2:**AMBITION**

PART 3: MIND AND BODY

PART 4: **VOICE**

<u>Zara:</u> So, this is the book, huh?

<u>Michelle:</u> I am fucking terrified. And excited! But mostly terrified. Am I supposed to say something important here? I feel lost. I have stage fright. My third word in our book is 'fucking'. I'm seeing little black dots everywhere. Help.

<u>Z:</u> Lest we lose the book deal before the book has even begun, let me get this underway with a question: Why? Why a book? Why now? Why at all?

<u>M:</u> Oh, that's easy. Why a book? Well, we wanted to write a book about the weird gap in life that's fuelled by cheap tacos and even cheaper tequila – also known as your twenties. It's when you're an adult, but not an *adult*-adult – the kind who is still intimidated by quince paste but can appreciate eclectic cushion arrangements at West Elm. It's a time when I've felt alone and confused; when a lot of shit has flown into my face (figuratively, and only once literally, if you count that seagull in 2018) and I haven't known what to do with any of it. I know you're the same, along with every other twenty-something I have ever met. So, we wrote a book about this specific limbo, in all its chaotic magic.

Z: This is true (the tequila, not the literal shit). Our twenties can be stupidly strange and it's not surprising that we are desperate to make sense of it all. I think so often during this phase of life we feel lost and confused, like we're in a constant and free-falling state of oblivion. Uncertainty can be paralysing, but it also can be illuminating. So, we wrote about all of it. We wrote about ourselves – our lives, our fears and our ambitions. We know you may not share our experiences, or that you may not relate to the specifics of our stories, but we hope, deeply, that you will be able to relate to the emotions we share. Fair?

M: Absolutely. And it's super important for Zara and me to say this upfront before we make you read 1500 of my very best words on the state of my fridge: we have written this book for every woman, but by virtue of being privileged, white, able-bodied, cisgendered, straight and middle-class, our experiences can't and won't be those of every woman.

Z: Our experience is not every experience, nor will we sit around and pretend the struggles we chose to write about are particularly cataclysmic. But we hope that when you read about them you might feel a tiny bit seen, or a tiny bit heard, or a tiny bit less alone.

M: We also want to be clear that this is not a how-to guide for your twenties. Why? Because we don't know shit, dummy! I only just figured out my car's petrol light has an arrow that tells me what side of the car to fill up on . . . and I only figured it out because Zara told me just then. So, as is abundantly clear, we have limited wisdom to offer you. For every kernel of clarity there's another question, conundrum or crossroads to plod through.

Z: We do not have the answers. Hell, we're only twenty-six as we write this. But our twenties (so far), in all their messy and unencumbered glory, are worth our time and exploration, no matter how frivolous or unimportant they are sometimes made out to be. They allow us to sift through the shit that doesn't matter so we can find the gems we care about. They are about reflecting on the space between who we were and who we are, and bridging the space between who we are now and who we intend to be. These twentysomething years are our building blocks, our personal puzzles, a time of mazes and boundless questioning.

<u>M:</u> Navigating the space between adolescence and true adulthood will see us encounter copious stumbles and fuck-ups along the way. For the first time in our lives, we're learning that we're not right about literally everything. Actually, there's this thing called a 'grey area', and another thing called 'nuance', and they'll show you that you're nowhere near as smart as you might think you are. But that's what makes this chapter of our lives so damn bewitching. This is when we get to explore and figure it all out, with a blueprint that doesn't quite look like anyone else's, with a destination we'll likely spend our whole lives trying to reach. It's wildly exciting, right? It might not feel like that right now, of course. You might be reading these words and feeling like your personal compass is pointing nowhere, other than to a future of bleary unknowns. That's okay too. You're not alone in feeling lonely and unsure.

<u>Z:</u> We wrote this book as an extension of our *Shameless* community. We wanted to create another place to tell stories, because stories are central in helping us map out our place in the world. This is the book we want you to read with your sisters and your girlfriends. This is for you, whoever you are or hope to be. We hope you find tiny pieces of yourself in the space between this page and the last one.

<u>M:</u> Too meta? Not meta enough? Good luck in there, kids. We'll see you on the other side.

29 amazing things about being single in your twenties

1. You can have sex with as many people as you damn well please.

2. You can have sex with as few people as you damn well please.

3. If you breathed a sigh of relief at number two, you're likely also saving time and money (and ingrown hairs from not shaving your sacred lady place).

4. Casual, everyday things are a little bit spicier for you than for your non-single mates. Your morning coffee comes with a side of *That barista was kind of cute.* You have a silent flirtation going on with that British trainer at the gym. The person sitting across from you on the tram swiped right on your Bumble profile last night.

5. You could meet a royal tomorrow! Or an actor! Or a famous musician! (You almost definitely won't, but you *could*.)

6. A vibrator is never going to break up with you.

7. Neither will Netflix.

8. Also, neither of these will cheat on you with a girl named Becky who has shitty hair extensions.

9. Attending weddings comes with an air of intrigue. And opportunity. And possibility.

10. Actually, *all nights out* come with an air of intrigue. And opportunity. And possibility.

11. You can slide into DMs.

12. You can pash (then ghost) whoever the fuck you want.

13. You can have sex with your university tutor. (We're not saying you should. We're just saying . . . you can. They might get fired but, like . . . you can.)

14. Drunken 2 am fights about who forgot to buy toilet paper are a foreign concept to you.

15. As are drunken 2 am fights about a very minor miscommunication that blew up into the Mount Vesuvius of relationship clusterfucks, for that matter.

16. You do not have to worry about impressing someone else's mum.

17. You do not have to share a bed with anybody. No middle-of-the-night knees in your back, or creepy deep breathing, or sleep talking. NO SNORING.

18. You can decorate your space/apartment/blimp (we don't know where you live) however you damn well please. Scented candles galore! Colourful cushions! A giant print of a native bird! More is more!

19. Cereal is a valid and worthy contender when you're weighing up Tuesday night dinner options.

20. You do not have to share your fries with anybody.

21. You do not have to share your sticky date pudding with anybody.

22. You do not have to share your bottle of wine with . . . you get the picture by now, right?

23. You do not have to factor anyone else in to your decision-making. Ever. (Kind of.)

24. SO MUCH FREE TIME to invest in yourself, your family, your friends, and that *Sims* addiction you keep telling yourself will end any day now.

25. You do not have to wait for anyone when you're bingeing a banger TV series.

26. You do not have to wait for anyone to GET READY FOR BRUNCH ALREADY on a Sunday morning because SOMEONE is hungover and SOMEONE is a turtle.

27. You do not have to go to the movies and see films you absolutely do not want to see. (*The Fast and the Furious*, we're looking at you. Also, Adam Sandler. Literally anything with Adam Sandler.)

28. You might move to London next month. Or Darwin. Or wherever the hell this crazy time in your life takes you, because you're living it for you, and only you, and there's something that feels awfully wide, wild and wonderful about that.

29. You have the space and freedom to actually get to know yourself, completely and fully. You realise that you're not just self-reliant, you're also smart and capable and pretty damn proud of the person you're becoming.

The space between heartbreak and healing

– ZARA –

The first time my heart broke, I was surprised by how much it hurt. How it battered my heart and bruised my chest, then obliterated my self-confidence, my resolve and every fragment of my sense of self.

I spent the days afterwards wondering what I'd done wrong, what I'd done to turn him off, and if perhaps I'd said something differently, we would still be together. I would look back and try to pinpoint the moment he decided we were done. Maybe if I'd noticed it then, I could've changed his mind in time?

The first time my heart broke, I was twenty years old. It was late, nearing midnight, and I remember driving home from his house in my tiny, cold, rattling car, dumbfounded that we were over. For the three years before that car ride home, we had been *us* – I had been his, he had been mine, our lives had been each other's. That night, he decided we were no longer us. I was no longer his, he was no longer mine.

It was the literal aspect of heartbreak that struck me most in the immediate aftermath of that conversation. My emotional pain manifested into physical pain, and I was blown away by how visceral it felt. My heart was heavy, as if it were sinking; the beat was irregular, as if the valves were constricting. My chest was full of tiny rocks, suffocated by an ache that seemed as if it would never subside.

I struggled to accept that the one who had been there all along, the one who had been there for it all, was suddenly no longer there at all. It felt like the most callous kind of subtraction equation: they were there and now they're not and all that's left at the end is you. Heartbreak, huh? The word made more and more sense as the crack in my heart began to separate and give birth to a chasm.

When we sat down to write this book, I knew I wanted to write about heartbreak. I wanted to write about the way it can consume your life when it happens in your twenties; how, when it strikes, it can feel like you may never recover. I asked questions of the women around me. What was it about heartbreak that surprised them the most? Where does their mind take them when they think of the moments they felt totally diminished by it?

The answers were varied, much like the women themselves, though the overarching themes were the same. Heartbreak is physical. It takes a toll on your body, after which it takes a long time to find and feel normal again. It makes you ache in a way that feels material, not just mental. Heartbreak is the shock of realising the sun will rise the next day and set some hours later, and that person still won't be by your side.

According to Sydney-based psychologist Jacqui Manning, we feel heartbreak so deeply because it's a strand of grief, a bereavement of its own kind.

'The feeling of love is extremely intoxicating and heady and strong, and I think when you have the flip side of that, which is saying goodbye to someone – even if it's a decision that you know in your bones is the right one for you – the feelings of sadness and grief are really palpable,' she says.

The thing about experiencing your first heartbreak now – and when we say 'now' we mean in this hyper-digitalised era – is that it's easy to avoid processing it, Manning says.

'Too often we try to avoid grief, but there's no shortcut through it. Allowing yourself to process it – by trying to talk it out or by crying or journalling – is really important now more than ever, because we live in a world where it's easy to be distracted. We do whatever it takes to take our mind off things, and while it's tempting or easy to do that, it won't make the grief go away. It's something to be lived through,' she says.

Another thing that struck me when talking to Manning was her theory that our generation questions our decision-making more than previous generations, thus compounding the anxiety that comes with heartbreak.

'In the world, there's so much choice. And with choice comes decisions and with decision-making comes anxiety,' she says.

So not only are we desperately sad but we're also really bloody confused. In our consumer-oriented, late-capitalist Western culture, we are faced with decisions all day, every day – and with indecision comes insecurity. After all, when there are too many choices, how can you possibly be sure the one you've made is the right one?

Her thoughts reminded me of the concept of FOBO ('fear of better options'), a social phenomenon conceived by Patrick McGinnis, an American venture capitalist who also coined the term FOMO back in 2003. But FOBO is about more than indecision: it's about a generation raised on the concept of choice, who are now paralysed when it comes to committing to decisions, both big and small, because we want to make the *best* decision, with only the most *perfect* outcome. We are terrified of unsatisfactory outcomes, and so we overthink: be it what we want for dinner, how we want to spend our Saturday nights or whether ending a relationship really is the best call.

Add this to the fact that, Manning says, our brains don't fully develop until the age of about twenty-five and you've got a recipe for messy, unprocessed feelings. Here we all are, dealing with adult issues that come with adult emotions at an age psychologists argue we aren't actually physically equipped for it. But perhaps it all comes down to experience: we can't process the emotion of heartbreak properly because it's something we've never been consumed by before.

'At that age, you don't have a reference point to know that things are going to be okay,' Manning says. 'You might go through heart-break half a dozen times in your life, but you will survive, you will move forward, you will find new meaning in your life. But at that early juncture, you don't really have a reference point for it.'

Which is to say, if you're in the depths of a broken heart right now, it's normal to feel like things have ruptured to the point of no return. But think of it this way: this rupture, the one that has flattened and nearly broken you, may well act as a valuable lesson for repair next time.

The second time my heart broke, I was surprised by how much it still hurt. How it battered my heart, bruised my chest and made me question who I was, who I was becoming and who I wanted to be. Even though this time I was the one who ended things, my heart still constricted and sank in the same way it did before, the blindside replaced by the dread of having to walk away. The disbelief overtaken by guilt.

The second time my heart broke, I was twenty-four years old.

It was evening, nearing sunset, and I remember driving home from his house in a newer but no-less-tiny car, dumbfounded that I had finally pulled the trigger. I called my best friend on the drive home and asked her if I was making the right choice, whether biting doubt was normal or if I was making the biggest mistake of my life. I remember asking her why, even though something had been off for a while and had been niggling at my subconscious for months, nothing in that moment felt absolute. It hadn't yet made total sense, and clarity wouldn't come for some time. The second time round, the motions felt much the same: sleep became fragmented, food became tasteless, the ground underneath me precarious, as if at any moment I could put a foot wrong and fall through the cracks.

There's a funny dialogue about heartbreak and its aftermath that characterises your early twenties. Friends have asked me since: would you rather be broken up with or do the breaking up? Would you rather have your heart broken or break a heart? The question always seemed reductive, because I felt that heartbreak, in any and all of its forms, exploded in a similar manner. Break a heart or have your own broken, it's all the same when you're left by your-self with your heart in your throat and your head in your hands. No one sits you down and explains how this sense of displacement will overwhelm you; that, for some time, you won't know where you fit or where you fall, or who to turn to. You will be plagued with feelings of disorientation, of feeling untethered; you will find yourself searching for something without shape, something you can't see. Searching for something you're not even sure exists.

No one tells you how desperate you will be for a time you're not so sad, confused, or completely unsure of yourself. That it's totally normal to have no desire to crane your neck and look back, but to just as equally feel paralysed when it comes to moving forward. They don't warn you you'll often turn to your phone, drunk, and realise, through blurry eyes and wobbly thumbs, that you're not sure who to text. That you will have to work through the minutiae of your day yourself, without palming off the tiny, inconsequential details to the person whose job it is to listen. That you will win and you will lose and you won't know who to call. That heartbreak is learning to embrace time: endless, still stretches of time. Time on a Friday night you have forgotten how to fill, time on a Sunday afternoon spent hungover with a mind that both wanders and wonders. *What next? What now?* It's getting home after a long week to no plans, and knowing a dark home and a dark room are yours alone to light up.

They don't warn you that heartbreak is also realising that you had better start liking yourself, because it's *you* who you'll be spending the most time with. It's learning to live with loneliness in all its forms rather than falling into the wrong arms for the sake of company. It's knowing that being alone, despite how much you hate it, is the fastest way to know and understand yourself. It's the moments you forget. The ones where you go to refer to them as your partner and not your ex, the moments you forget that you're a single entity and not a package deal. It's the moments where you forget all the reasons you're alone to begin with.

It's all of those things, but it's also so much more.

It's the euphoria of catching yourself in the moments in which you're feeling okay, your shit is together and you realise it's been a couple of days since you've traced their every step on social media. It's moving through the world with the freedom to fill your own cup and serve your own soul, of looking at those endless stretches of time and having the power to do with them what you want. Of knowing that loving and losing is in the blueprint of your years, and recognising that there aren't many humans who haven't felt heartbreak like sandpaper to the soul. It's sitting amongst love, of being in the presence of others in love and knowing you'll get it back.

The next question I asked the women around me, in particular the thousands of women in our podcast community, was this: what did the throes of heartbreak teach you, as you worked desperately to claw your way out of it?

The answers came in a flurry and I found, once again, that though the women were as complex and varied as their stories, their conclusions felt familiar. They learned to be content with who they are and what they have, they discovered that it took time to notice what toxic behaviours were infiltrating their relationships, and that sometimes love can stifle you to the point where you don't know who you are anymore. And that heartbreak can also be freeing. Nothing encourages you to say yes to things – to yourself, your friends and terrifying opportunities – more than a splintered heart.

Jacqui Manning says there is validity to the line of thought that your twenties are a great time to muddle your way through heartbreak because you are more emotionally available than perhaps you'll ever be. No, you're not as mature and no, you don't yet have those reference points to know that things will eventually heal, but what you do have are the time, energy and space to process your feelings in a way you may never be able to again.

'You think you're really busy at different times in your life, and then you realise as challenges come up and you start to grow or you even have kids, that actually, time does shrink. In your twenties, you do have more time to process it all.'

It's that concept of freedom, Manning argues, that we should be harnessing when our youth overlaps with our sadness. Feeling heartbroken and having time doesn't have to be a double-pronged death wish.

'Your twenties are when you are trying heaps of stuff out – whether that is relationships or a bunch of other things – and while you do know yourself to a degree, I think you're learning what you like [and] what you don't like, and you've got the freedom to try it all. Your focus gets a little narrower as you get older. Sure, there are a lot of questions rather than answers in your twenties, but the flipside of that is that it comes with an enormous amount of freedom.'

Of course, the great irony of feeling both free and heartbroken in your twenties is the impatience that comes with looking for answers and waiting to feel better again. For a generation raised on the principles of immediacy (for one, it's never been easier to order food and have it on your doorstep twenty minutes later), we're desperate for results and we're desperate for them now. But you can't skip the days or the chapters or the pain. You have no choice but to move through every spike, feel every twinge and nurse every wound.

Manning says the answers will come, so long as we are willing to self-reflect. To be blunt: being blind to the role you may have played in inducing your own heartbreak is unhelpful, and may well be a hindrance to your future and future relationships.

'If there's one thing I'd encourage people in their twenties to do when it comes to relationships [it's] to read and learn about their own family dynamics, because that does play out in their own relationships. It all comes up, and it's important you're not driven by your subconscious, that you don't keep choosing partners that might not be suited to you,' she says.

Heartbreak isn't beautiful, not even with hindsight. Heartbreak is gritty and messy and full of fury and anguish. It's not clean, nor is the path to moving past it. To assume we will become wonderful versions of ourselves in the process of grappling with it is to be deluded because no one is the best version of themselves in sadness. Heartbreak is just a litmus test, a way to check yourself and a way to check in with yourself, an opportunity to decide what you want moving forward and the person you want to be throughout it.

'If you're in intense pain, it's important to see what you can learn from that, even if it's hard to stop and think,' Manning says. 'What did you do in that relationship that wasn't great, that wasn't healthy? You'll learn something through self-reflection, and give yourself the opportunity to do things differently next time. That said, reading about heartbreak is not the same as experiencing it. Unfortunately, the experience of heartbreak is all part of the package, as is falling in love the next time.'

The thing about self-reflection is that often, it doesn't come when you're mired right in deep pain. It comes when the clouds have cleared and your heart feels a little lighter, when you look back and then you look forward and you realise that wisdom is now inside you. When you realise your eyes aren't so glassy, your brain isn't so foggy and *hey*, the sky is starting to look a little blue again.

When I fell in love while nursing a fractured heart, I wasn't prepared for how much it would disorientate my mind and mess with my bearings. I couldn't believe how quickly I became so invested in someone else, so excited about a future with another human, and yet was still so totally captured by the nostalgia of the years gone by. The first time I fell in love while nursing a fractured heart, I was twenty-five years old.

The first thing I noticed about him was his laugh; how when he found something funny he wouldn't just smile, or his eyes wouldn't just light up, but he would throw his head forward and let it fall out of him. I remember – or, to be more accurate, I hardly remember – sitting with him over dinner that first time, utterly inebriated because I was terrified to start dating again. I remember trying not to baulk as he ordered us prawns, because who makes someone shell a giant prawn the first time you meet them? I noticed how every square centimetre of his being felt safe, as if no matter which way he turned or the angle he faced or how wide his arms stretched, he'd likely be protecting me from something before I knew I needed it. I remember little except sitting by his side as more than eight hours passed, wondering who this person was and where he had always been.

I had no intention of ever leaving that first date, of ever leaving him altogether, and a wave of shyness washed over me as we said goodbye because I'd spent less time with him than I'd usually work in a day and already I was thinking that maybe this was the person I'd end up with.

I remember the terror of those early dates. I'd accidentally found myself so invested in someone I hardly knew, and I was surprised by the ease with which I could imagine myself with him, and he with me, and us together. I was frightened by the thought of losing him before I had the opportunity to properly get to know him. I'd found someone far kinder, far funnier and far more easygoing than I. How was I going to hold on to that?

I remember all of that – feeling full and content and hopeful and frightened – but still feeling the pull of the ones who had come before, as if I owed something to the one whose heart I had broken and the one who had broken mine.

Maybe the saying is true; maybe if you've loved someone once you'll probably love them (in a different form) forever. Maybe it doesn't make you any less excited for the future or any less invested in the space you now find yourself in, but maybe it just makes you human.

There's a reason heartbreak hurts so deeply, a reason it ruptures your soul and your sense of self, too. Maybe it's meant to scar you, maybe that's the point of the pain, and maybe you'll learn to grow from that. Because from the scars and the pain and hindsight comes the best possible understanding of yourself – of the space between who you were, who you are and who you intend to be.

That battered heart of yours will find a way to mend, that much I now know. Those sleepless nights, those waves of shock, those indiscriminate floods of loneliness will eventually disappear and that bruised chest will piece itself back together, even if it looks a little different. And when it does, you will look at the space between who you were at first heartbreak and who you are now, and marvel at how it was you – and only you – who managed to fill your own void.

The space between friends with benefits and a monogamous relationship

– MICHELLE –

If casual sex arrangements were a sugary cocktail and serious relationships were a hearty main course, situationships – AKA the space between 'friends with benefits' and 'monogamous relationship' – would be a moreish pre-dinner snack.

Think of anything that gives you the comfort of a proper dinner, without a sliver of the nutritional content. Say, chunky buttered slices of bread! Chocolate-covered pretzels! Or those twiggy stick thingy-ma-bobs! (An important disclaimer so nobody gets lost in the metaphor – We all good? Still with me? – situationship snacks are *moderation foods*, the stuff you find at the very top of those 'healthy-eating pyramid' posters on the walls of school canteens, or mentioned in studies on colon cancer.)

Now, the key to nibbling your way through a situationship is mindfulness. You must put down the bread/pretzels/twiggy sticks before they hurt your stomach and ruin your life. This is Very Important because if you're not careful you'll grow convinced that you can stop thinking about dinner altogether because you're happy

LOVE

as a clam right here, elbow-deep in this bag of ambiguous salty meat poles, wondering if they're still sleeping with other people.

You see, the twiggy sticks take you on cute picnic dates and deliver your favourite chocolate bars to your work, but they also refuse to introduce you to their friends or family. They talk about their future with the inference that you'll be in it, but simultaneously give off the impression that *yes, they're absolutely still sleeping with other people.*

But it's too late. It's been eight weeks, and it dawns on you that you want the twiggy sticks to be your main course. You want them to be yours, just as you realise there are no more twiggy sticks left. You are in love with the impossibly bad twiggy sticks but they have vanished, never to be seen again until they pop up on your Instagram feed with their arms dangling around that pretty girl from your cousin's media studies class.

Yeah, that's a situationship.

For a long time, the grey situationship blob was my thing. I found that dating someone for two-to-four months was the sweet spot – that way, you could break through the awkward barrier of 'our teeth sometimes clang when we kiss' without finding yourselves smack bang in Boredomville, on a monotonous loop of mediocre documentaries and white-bread sex. One month of dating and you end up with spine-tingling embarrassment every time you see them on a night out. Five months and one of you has absolutely caught feelings. But two to four? You're in the clear. You did that situationship thing right, my friend. Bravo. Twiggy sticks for all.

Sometimes I got it right. Other times, I got it catastrophically wrong.

Let's see, shall we?

There was the guy who only paid for $5 top-ups of petrol at a time because he'd always blown all his money the night before on cigarettes and ecstasy pills. We dated for a few months when I was eighteen. If I saw him today I'd feel sentimental and think of the early days – the movie dates, all that frozen yogurt. Then I'd be bowled over by a tsunami of The Ick.

There was the professional athlete I dated on and off for a few months, whose ego was so *impressive* that conversations about socks weren't safe from the name-dropping of C-grade celebrities. If I saw him today I'd feel pretty good, considering I ended things and therefore have the upper hand forevermore. Ha.

Then. Oh, reader, *then*. Then there was the dude who perennially smelled of carrot, celery and chicken thigh because that's what he insisted on eating for breakfast (!!!) every morning. Here comes the real clincher, though: I fell in love with him, like a bona fide gold-star idiot. It still makes me ashamed to admit it, all these years later. Thinking back, the main reason was that I liked his floppy hair quite a bit. And his taste in music. Also, memes. Boy did he know his way around a good meme. You see, he was impossibly charming over text – smart, dry and funny all at once. We dated for five months before he suddenly stopped replying to my messages and calls. A few weeks later he was Facebook Official with a girl he met at a music festival. I cried a lot over him. It took months to not freeze every time I saw a floppy-haired guy buying chicken thighs at the supermarket. It took even longer to restore my sense of confidence, to stop wondering why he picked her over me – to feel like myself again. If I saw him today, despite all the years that insulate me from that experience, and all the impenetrable love I have for my boyfriend, I would still feel pangs of hollowness. Not because I hold any shred of affection for him, but because he showed me just how romantic rejection can feel like your ribcage is a microwave, slowly melting the organs behind your bones.

Chicken Thigh Guy showed me that having the perks of a conventional relationship (Cute dates! Not-terrible sex! Goodnight text messages!) while not having the boundaries of one (Please don't smush your genitals with other people!) can lead to disaster.

Situationships brim with goosebumpy excitement and face-numbing doubt. They can make you feel alive and broken in equal measure. Shiny and special one second, totally forgettable the next.

Their name popping up on your phone screen makes you feel wanted, like you're seen, like you matter. You begin to recognise the contours of their couch, their bed, their body, without ever knowing if those spaces are filled by someone else when you're not around. You lie between their sheets and hear about their childhood, of moments that shaped their existence before you ever stepped into it. If you slip, you'll start to think of this person as *your* person when they belong to nobody, especially not to you.

You live life in the nows – the next hour, the next dinner date, the next afternoon spent in bed watching a Louis Theroux documentary – but never the next week or month.

You'll feel them pull away gently – just a little – at first. It's so imperceptible that the most rational and reasonable part of you dismisses it as nothing; as forgetfulness, a busy work schedule, sickness. The commotion of life. Sure, they only work ten hours a week at General Pants, but maybe lots of people are buying flared jeans right now! And moody jumpers! And festival backpacks!

The panic rises when you realise you've broken the only rule you ever made with yourself: *Don't get feelings*. It's too late. The feelings are there, and they turn tender whenever a text goes without a reply or a day passes without communication. Within a week, the Rational You can no longer calm the Emotional You – the foundation of what this is has shifted beneath your feet without you even realising, and that movie they told you they so desperately wanted to see with you? They've just seen it with someone else.

You can't raise the alarm, of course, because they're not your partner and they owe you nothing. Don't be needy, now. Nobody likes a needy girl, haven't you heard? Maybe they just wanted a bit of space, you tell yourself. Maybe things really have been so helplessly hectic that they couldn't find twenty-five seconds in their busy day to send you a message asking about yours. The dates you once went on are replaced by suggestions of last-minute hook-ups. There are no messages outside those sent in a typo-laden flurry between Friday at 10 pm and Sunday at 4 am.

And then there's nothing at all.

Sometimes, you'll be lucky to receive a text explaining why they lost interest. Mostly, all you'll have is space – a sudden absence, a silence – and you'll be tasked with filling in all the blanks. *Was it me? Was there something missing? Have I been replaced?*

You will read through old messages that insisted you mattered. You will also pore over social media accounts that suggest the total opposite is true. Because if you mattered, why were you kept a secret? If you mattered, why did they grow bored so swiftly? If you mattered, why don't they care?

And that's where the brutal truth lies: you were a parenthesis in that chapter of their life. You made them a protagonist in yours, of course. To you, they were the person around whom everything else moved. You thought about them when you went to sleep and when you woke, when your boss gave you orders to do that stocktake count, or your housemate asked you to cling-wrap the leftovers from dinner. You imagined what it would be like to do things for real, to stop playing pretend and actually make your relationship something concrete and tangible. All that energy, just to end up as nothing more than a parenthesis: easily ignored, forgotten, deleted.

There are no photos of you together on social media. No mutual friends who can vouch for the electric current that flowed between you. There is no proof of what you had other than the streams of blue and grey bubbles on your phone, the only evidence of what was once there and now isn't.

You've lost someone who wasn't quite a friend, but wasn't quite a boyfriend. *And how the hell do you explain that loss to the people around you?*

Friends and family won't understand the cataclysmic shift. Situationships aren't typically concrete enough to be recognised by those who aren't inside them. Maybe the person you fell in love with never met any of your favourite people. Maybe they didn't try to see you out in the real world at all. Maybe they never imprinted themselves on your life, just the parts of you that you don't quite understand yet.

You'll watch romantic comedies that will warn you away from this kind of love, movies that scream, 'He's just not that into you!' and tell you to get a haircut, or a cat, or both. You'll finally understand why Taylor Swift wrote all those songs about Jake Gyllenhaal when they dated for all of five minutes. You'll grow to understand Taylor Swift circa 2012 a lot, actually. You'll play 'All Too Well' on repeat. You'll read blog posts that tell you this ache in your chest is a blessing, that bigger and better things are coming, that they're only around the corner. Only you don't want 'bigger' or 'better'. You just want what you had. You just want them to want you.

~

The world might not recognise what happened to you in a situationship, but *you should*. You might still think about them for years to come, not because you still want them – you'll soon learn that you deserve so much better than what they gave you – but because they showed you just how great things can be. They showed you just how fucking painful they can be, too. That pain might linger for a long time and that's okay. You're not the first person to fall for a twiggy-stick jerk who didn't appreciate just how wonderful and funny and bright you are.

One day, the right person will come along and they will be your safe harbour. And without this experience, you mightn't have learned how to spot them.

So for now, just think: if love can be that fizzy and bubbly with a person who won't commit to you, imagine how effervescent it will be with someone who gently cradles your heart in their hands, and offers you theirs in return.

You've only had a taste of what is coming.

And trust me: the main course? It's even more wonderful than you can imagine.

LOVE

A basic bitch's guide
to the basic-bitch guys
you'll have sex with in
your twenties

In an ideal world, you'll be having sex with *far more interesting people* in your twenties. If you're anything like the typical straight twenty-something, though? You'll be wasting at least a year or two on these peanuts . . .

	The guy everyone insists is a 'good bloke'	The stoner
Ambitions	Seems to have spent the last eight years doing a three-year commerce degree because he decides to complete two subjects a semester. Will likely never use said degree because his parents will find him a job anyway.	Look, dunno, but he smokes weed a lot, loves going to dust-ridden festivals even more, and seems hell-bent on finding ways to make lots of money while putting in no actual effort.
Personality	Funny, which is annoying. Charming enough that it'll distract you from the fact he hasn't held down a relationship (Situationship? Neither?) for longer than six weeks. Will tag you in memes because he's under the illusion that this is an adequate substitute for real-life communication (it isn't).	So chill about you and his life in general that you're not actually sure if he's conscious. Has a remarkable ability to go on benders that no human body should be able to withstand. Your mother *would literally kill you* if she knew you were having sex with this human being. He's nice, though.
Quality of sex, as illustrated by his iconic movie character alter ego	Nate from *The Devil Wears Prada*: On first impression, he seems good! Great, in fact! But then, as his true colours begin to shine through, you realise he is a bit of a one-trick pony who, despite pushing your head into his lap at every opportunity, doesn't reciprocate oral sex.	Ben Stone from *Knocked Up*: Pretty boring, to be honest. You secretly harbour suspicions that he has marijuana-induced erectile dysfunction but he's way too relaxed to even care, so you decide to fake it every time so he doesn't feel bad. (And by 'every time' we mean, like, four times before you never see each other again, because fuck that.)
Inevitable outcome	He will ruin your life. You will fall in love with this dickhead but he won't want to date properly because he's 'moving overseas soon'. One week after you stop texting, he'll announce his new relationship on Facebook with that girl he told you not to worry about.	You will slowly ghost each other, but you'll always wonder if he actually ever ghosted you or just totally forgot you existed.

	The guy from your Sail Croatia boat	The AFL player (or the guy who is still trying to become one)
Ambitions	Don't remember.	His life goal is to get invited to the Brownlow, to which he'd absolutely invite his mother and not you because you, *my special little snowflake*, are merely one out of the nine women he is casually sleeping with right now. Also, bringing his mum is great for his personal brand.
Personality	Don't know.	He's nice and all, but likes to name-drop every celebrity whose number is in the contacts list on his phone. Brags about getting invited to the Birdcage at the Spring Racing Carnival at every opportunity. Is verified on Instagram even though he has like 3000 followers.
Quality of sex, as illustrated by his iconic movie character alter ego	Don't remember.	John Tucker from *John Tucker Must Die*: First of all, don't ask us why, but this guy always – ALWAYS – has a name that starts with the letter 'J'. It's just a fact of life, kind of like grapefruit being the worst fruit in human history. We digress. He is decent in bed, has a good body, and knows his way around yours because he's slept with half of the women in your local area.
Inevitable outcome	Nothing, obviously.	A one-night stand that turns into twelve to twenty-four months of Saturday night Snapchats. Text messages never go beyond *Hey! Yeah not much, how about you?* territory and *What are you up to?* at 1 am on said Saturday nights.

The guy who 'likes' conservative newspaper articles	The guy who thinks his career and ambitions are far more serious than yours	
He told you what he does for work on your first date but you were four rosés deep, so you're still tossing up between carpenter and construction manager. Or maybe a cameraman? Hmmm. Who knows! He spends a lot of time doing CrossFit, so there's that.	Whatever they are, yours COULDN'T POSSIBLY COMPARE! Look at his suit. At his shiny, shiny shoes. Has he mentioned he has that client presentation tomorrow morning?	Ambitions
Boisterous. The life of the party, always. Is so sarcastic online that you're not quite sure if he's making fun of trolls, or is actually just a troll himself. Refers to women as 'birds' and his friends' partners as 'the misso'. Also has about three too many gambling apps on his phone.	Textbook mansplainer. Will tell you exactly how to do your job (even if you're in health care and he's in banking). See also: where to invest your money (even though he only invested in Bitcoin when it went mainstream).	Personality
Ben Barry from How to Lose a Guy in 10 Days: You suspect all of his sexual education came from porn, given his idea of good sex is sweatily jackhammering you for one minute and twenty-five seconds before turning over and sleeping.	Zane Anders from Younger: You know exactly what this guy is like in bed, as if we need to tell you.	Quality of sex, as illustrated by his iconic movie character alter ego
You have a vague, long-running suspicion that he has a tendency to be racist/sexist/homophobic, only it's so vague that it takes you months to conclude with any certainty that he is, in fact, racist, sexist, and homophobic. The trifecta! This realisation dawns on you when you sit down to watch a game of women's footy together.	Um. You don't really want to talk about it .... Okay fine, you saw him last night.	Inevitable outcome

The guy who is literally too nice for his own good

Ambitions

The manager of a bar, shop or cafe. Trustworthy and hard-working. Would nominate himself to clean out the gutters of your grandmother's home if it meant you'd notice him.

Personality

Insists on using an Android phone. Gives you way too many compliments, which is strange, because you love compliments. Reacts with a love heart or flame emoji on every Instagram story you upload. Replies to a photo you upload of your mum with a comment along the lines of 'Ah! And now I see where you get it from ;)'

Quality of sex, as illustrated by his iconic movie character alter ego

Jack from *Titanic:* Meh. It's fine. Lots of basic sex and cringe-worthy dirty talk. You know that he'd plunge himself into the icy depths of the Atlantic Ocean for you, despite you having plenty of room for him to climb aboard your door/life-raft. Literally everything about that is a total turn-off.

Inevitable outcome

You will break his heart and he'll tell you as much in an understandably savage text message after you flake out for the third time this month. You'll feel pangs of guilt about the way you treated him for the next four years.

A rough and tumble on ...
settling

On Tue, 21 Jan 2020 at 12:55 PM,
Michelle Andrews <michelleandrews@shameless.com> wrote:

>>> Z!

I think it would be stupid of us to do an entire bloody section on love without touching on the very real panic of settling – that niggling feeling that something just *isn't totally right* when it comes to your relationship with your significant other, and that maybe something bigger and better is out there.

So, let's start with you. You've had a couple of serious long-term relationships – have you ever had that dawning realisation that maybe the love you had for your partner just ... wasn't enough?

On Tue, 21 Jan 2020 at 1:13 PM,
Zara McDonald <zaramcdonald@shameless.com> wrote:

>>> I have indeed. Do you remember when we put a call out on Instagram for stories from young women who were in relationships that weren't enough? It was when we were recording early episodes of *Love Etc.* (the dating and relationships podcast that we produced in conjunction with Bumble Australia) and I remember so many people replied not with

stories, but with a question: when you find out what settling looks like, can you tell us?

I've ended happy, fulfilling relationships before because of a feeling that it just wasn't right. I would not say I have had a firm 'dawning realisation' moment, but with hindsight, I can see there was a build-up of tiny niggles that were probably telling me all along this was not my future.

They were omnipresent – always hovering in the background, sometimes dormant, sometimes fiery. *Love comes with niggles*, I told myself. You know, that it's normal to look to your future and wonder if they will be there, or to see an engagement announcement and think, *Would I feel that happy too?*

The thing about being in a romantic relationship is that while you're still in it, you may never really know with one hundred per cent certainty if you're settling. That realisation can only really come from a bird's-eye view, a vantage point that necessitates separation and space from your partner. Only you can discover it for yourself. No one can explain to you what's worth your worry, no one can paint you a picture, no one can point to a part of your relationship and say, *Hey, see that part there? That's the one you should be worrying about.* I couldn't even articulate how I was feeling, either. But it wasn't that I couldn't put into words what was wrong and why it was wrong, it was more that I couldn't shake the inverse of that: not everything felt *right*, and that, in itself, felt wrong.

And then, as fast as the doubts arose, I shot them down, telling myself this was love, of course: it ebbs and it flows. Real love is grounded in reality: your blinkers aren't on, your love isn't blind. I told myself I was being selfish, I was asking for too much. What if good enough is enough? What if the grass isn't greener? What if I'm just being picky?

In the years since, I've realised that love should not come with that many questions. The kind of self-justification that consumed me – the kind that was weighing up the positives and negatives, that always encouraged me to remember the good times rather than focus on the doubts – was a red flag. I now wonder if the niggles were trying to tell me something.

They kept coming and going because they were trying to tell me that if the relationship was enough, I wouldn't be asking myself the question.

What about you? Do you think sometimes you need to be in a relationship that's not quite enough to understand what more than enough looks like?

On Tue, 21 Jan 2020 at 1:39 PM,
Michelle Andrews <michelleandrews@shameless.com> wrote:

>>> I'm not sure you need to be in a *relationship* that's 'not enough' to understand what settling feels like. The beauty of dating lots of people in your teens and twenties without lasting commitment is that you get a taste of other lives; although, nibbling on someone's head and promptly deciding they're not your Cup-of-Life Partner can be a little brutal. But hey, welcome to dating! Take a condom. Take five.

Before I was with Mitch, I was the definition of picky. I could spend months dating someone and be turned off them irreparably at the whiff of a spicy cologne. I flaked out on dates at the last minute for no real reason at all, other than the fact I couldn't be fucked spending three hours at a tapas restaurant when I had already decided it would go nowhere and leave us both $50 poorer. I was picky because on some level, I felt all the niggles that told me those guys weren't right for me. We probably could have had quite happy relationships together, but in every instance, something was just slightly . . . off, and in dating them, I had been settling all along. At the time, I would blame my decision to walk away on something odd and tiny, like the aforementioned stench of their cinnamon-y fragrance, but I know now that Mitch could bathe in a tub of that stuff and I'd still want to kiss his face the moment I wake up.

For me right now, the question of 'Are you settling?' is an easy one to answer.

I know that I'm not settling because the thought of losing my relationship is sickening. Despite whatever today holds, I know with absolute certainty that the highlight will be seeing my boyfriend walk through the door at the end of it all. I know that I tell him 'I love you' so many times a day I lose count. I know that when I think of 'home' I don't think of a place, I think of him. The answer to the 'Are you settling?' question will either be a 'No', or a pause while you confront the uncomfortable reality that something intangible and important might be missing.

On Tue, 21 Jan 2020 at 2:00 PM,
Zara McDonald <zaramcdonald@shameless.com> wrote:

>>> It's interesting you say that. I'll never forget the conversation I had with my best friend just minutes after I ended a relationship that defined much of my early adult years. She was based in London and living through my pain via an occasionally crackly WhatsApp line. I told her I wished I was one hundred per cent sure breaking up was the right thing to do, rather than the thirty to forty per cent I was hovering at. I'll never forget her warm but firm voice barrelling down the line.

'Zara,' she said, 'being thirty to forty per cent sure you want to leave is as much doubt as you need.'

In that second I knew she was right. You can never be totally sure, but doubt is your life raft, your sign. It's the thing you cling to in the moments that come later when you wonder if you made the right call.

Fear of leaving isn't the same as having a deep desire to stay. For so long, I'd justified my need to stay in relationships by referencing the fear I felt about leaving. But being scared of a life without a partner, of not knowing what my life looked like alone, wasn't enough to stay there forever. It wasn't indicative of a healthy relationship, but instead of habit, of attachment, of an inability to see myself as anything other than an extension of them. For so long I thought love was a comfortable thing: love was knowing them inside out, love was knowing who they were and who they would likely become. Love was in your shared history, in the story, in your longstanding commitment to each other, in the knowledge that your bond has been cemented over long stretches of uninterrupted time. But love needs to be more than routine and more than history.

Good love, I've since learned, is about more than wanting to love them. Good love doesn't make you question if you're settling or if it's enough. It is big enough to speak and stand for itself, and so the questions never come. Or in your mind, is that too wildly simplistic?

On Tue, 21 Jan 2020 at 2:18 PM,
Michelle Andrews <michelleandrews@shameless.com> wrote:

>>>   I love that. You know me: I am as soppy and romantic as they come.

I do want to dive into one thing you wrote, though, and tease it out a little bit: 'Good love doesn't make you question if you're settling or if it's enough. It is big enough to speak and stand for itself, and so the questions never come.'

It's important for us to acknowledge that, even if you are experiencing the good kind of love, that question of settling might still present itself, and that's okay, too.

Doubts might pop up, not because the relationship is doomed but because you're human. 'Good love' might not always *feel* good, especially when life is thrown off course. There will be speed bumps and tsunamis, and the sky might crack open with rain tomorrow. Grief, illness and loss might threaten to tug you apart. Your relationship might stumble in the face of those obstacles. You might hurt each other. You might do things you regret really, really deeply. Your hearts might bruise from the trauma. And yes, you might pause to wonder if this is where you want to be, and this is the person you want to be with. You might need some time to seriously ruminate on those questions. That's okay. There is no one-size-fits-all approach to love. This is all a balancing act, and it can be a damn hard one at that.

I think what I find interesting about the idea of settling now, more than four years into a relationship and three years into living together, is that you *will* go through patches of confusion. You will be challenged and you'll challenge your partner over and over again. Your differences will make you question what sacrifices you are willing to make for the person you love, and what catches in your throat. Whatever your answer to the question 'Are you settling?' is right now, it doesn't need to be your relationship's hamartia.

Suspecting you are, in fact, settling in your relationship doesn't mean the love is wrong or bad. Confronting it could mean that you have a chance to pivot – that you find your voice and can point to exactly what's missing, and ask for exactly what you need. The question could actually be the best thing to happen to your relationship because it could give your partner the opportunity to grow and deliver the kind of love you crave, the kind that will turn your answer into a resolute 'no' again.

Not every single day will be sunshiney. Hell, some months might be so dark you don't know how to get through them. But if you try to be each other's torch in those moments, then I think you're onto something really, truly great.

Which brings me back to you. First of all, do you think what I've said in this email is fair? And then, what would you say to someone reading this who not only suspects that maybe they are settling, but that their relationship is actually beyond repair?

On Tue, Jan 21 2020 at 2:45 PM,
Zara McDonald <zaramcdonald@shameless.com> wrote:

>>> I think that's absolutely fair. The hardest line to toe here is the knowledge that relationships are hard, but a relationship should never be *too* hard. Here's the thing, right (and it brings me back to the point I made earlier on): no one can create a watertight definition of a relationship that cannot, will not or should not go the distance. That's for us, individually, to decide. Certainly, you or I can't design a prototype of what settling looks like over the course of a few choice words.

I agree wholeheartedly that raising unhappiness in a relationship in a gentle and thoughtful way can be so telling. I've had times when I have been unhappy, and talking about that discontent has seen one of two outcomes: either they embrace you and your disquiet, or they don't. Either they commit to making changes, or they get defensive. Both of those outcomes have told me heaps about the future of that relationship. Raising it has been helpful.

To your point on the simplicity of me saying good love should come without the questions, I think what I mean is that good love should not come with the question of it ever being *enough*. I really do stand by that. That's not to say you might not wonder what life is like without them, or it's not to say moments won't feel bleak, but it's just to say, through all the monotony and tough times, if you are spending your time wondering if this is enough, then I think that is a problem.

When I was twenty-four and came to the realisation that I was willing to settle for not enough because I didn't know what more than enough looked like, I stumbled on a quote from the psychiatrist Carl Jung. I was squashed into an overcrowded bus as it weaved through Prague on a rainy, miserable day. *Until you make the unconscious conscious, it will direct your life and you will call it fate.*

It planted a seed, I think, because it was the first time I was forced to confront the niggles and doubt that had been fermenting over many months. My stomach started to flip, just a tiny bit. Over the coming weeks, it felt like my stomach was sinking into itself. It was a manifestation of dread, and it was strange, because I'd never known dread to pack such a punch. Up until this point, I had experienced dread in its most innocent, baby form: when you dread a meeting or a first date, a hard conversation or big goodbye. But I hadn't experienced it in such a consuming way.

I was confused. I wasn't unhappy, the relationship didn't feel broken, I didn't feel caged or stifled and I was still in love. I just simply couldn't shake the feeling that something wasn't right. So I guess if I were to say anything to the person who feels they are where I once was, I would say this: your twenties are a time of profound confusion – it's no surprise that our inbox was flooded all those months ago with women's questions about settling. If no one can tell you what settling is, or what it looks like for you, all you can do is back yourself. None of us knows if we are with our ideal 'soulmate', or if that guy buying potatoes next to us at Coles is actually a better fit.

I remember my sister once asked me, 'If you could end the relationship now and fast forward four months, past the stages of raw pain, would you do it?' It crystallised something important: I wasn't terrified of a life without them, I was terrified of a break-up, and all the discomfort that entails. Because if you're searching for your soulmate in the eyes of someone who isn't your partner, I think you need to listen to that voice inside you. Decipher what she's trying to say. She might be trying to tell you the truth.

Everything a global pandemic taught us about friendship

- 'The Space Between' will become *more literal than you had hoped* when you first pitched this book concept to your publisher.

- You don't have fifteen super close friends. Your actual circle is more like two to five people. And that's okay, because as shitty as this situation is, it's shown you who your people are. This tight little huddle of yours is secure and safe.

- Friendships don't have to be built on foundations of crazy drunken stories from nights out. Many are erected on the quiet building blocks of loyalty and time. Also, good books, good TV shows and good movies.

- No single person can be everything for you. You need different people for different things, especially when life is turned upside down.

- People will cope with trauma *very differently*. You will have at least one friend who is in complete denial, and another who is a connoisseur of conspiracy theories. Be gentle and patient with both.

- The people around you are trying to cope in the ways they know how. Even if you don't understand – or are disappointed – with how your friends behave, remember that they are doing their best.

- Playing the role of a good and caring friend is incredibly fulfilling when the walls of your collective worlds begin to crumble. Being loyal and kind – whether through sending them books or quotes or check-in messages – gives you a sense of purpose, too.

- There's something kind of lovely about calling a friend to check in and realising they no longer ask you why you're calling.

- The insecurity that you may be doing friendship wrong dissipates when there aren't as many means of comparison (AKA when you don't spend your Sunday mornings scrolling through Instagram watching back-to-back Boomerangs of people clinking wine glasses).

- You can't measure love. There is no metric for trust, loyalty, compassion, memories or laughter. The beauty and grit of friendship does not always shine through the virtual reality of your Instagram feed. Love exists outside these performative places, in the space between you and them and them and you.

- Your group chat becomes particularly chaotic when an emergency press conference interrupts *Married at First Sight* at 8 pm on a Sunday and forces you to grapple with how 'essential' or 'essentially unessential' your respective jobs are.

- There's a certain magic that's spun when you spend time with the people you love, all sprawled around a couch, or seated at a table, or jammed in the car. That energy can't be bottled, and it certainly can't be replicated in a video chat. Savour that buzz when it becomes your reality again.

- You miss, so much, being able to sit at a bar with your friends and watch them bounce off each other, knowing you don't have to be an active participant in the conversation to feel buoyed by it.

- Friendship is a salve for just about anything you will face in life. There will be hurdles that scare you and daunt you, and occasions when you're not sure you have the energy to even try, but that's what makes your friends so brilliant – the good ones will always be there, cheering from the sidelines as gently or aggressively as you need.

LOVE

The space between being a good friend and a bad one

– MICHELLE –

When I think of the greatest heartbreak of my twenties, I don't think of a boy who made me cry into the hollow pit of an ice cream tub. Instead, I think of a gradual stretching feeling. I think of curt text messages that never received replies. I think of phone calls that were intentionally left to run to voicemail. I think of staring into each other's faces at 3 am on a Sunday morning and silently asking, *When did we change? When did we become such totally different people? When did this snarkiness slither into every interaction we have?* I think of nights in bed spent on Facebook, Instagram, Twitter, LinkedIn, sleuthing with a particularly cautious thumb. *What is she doing now? Did she end up finishing that university course? Is . . . is she . . . wearing my top? Who's that bearded guy in her latest photo? What shade of lipstick is that? How's her mum? Is that seafood in her pasta? I thought she hated prawns? Since when does she like prawns?*

I don't think of a boy, because while boys have turned my heart shades of purple and blue, the greatest heartbreak stories I have are the friendship kind: the kind that made my heart grey. The romantic relationships I have lost with boys didn't carry the same complexities, or force me to grapple with the ugly reality that a friend who's like a sister can turn into a stranger in a matter of months. I look back at myself at nineteen and notice that the people who were around me then are different to the ones around me now. Some people are missing. People who, for a time, knew everything about me, and I about them.

I've lost friends. A best friend, even. She was my 'person'. The one I cackled with until I couldn't breathe. The one who saw me vomit stomachfuls of vodka cranberry into dingy club toilets beneath flickering lights. Who showed me the power of push-up bras – a power you really only care about for a fleeting window of three years, between the ages of seventeen and twenty. She knew how I liked my hair and did it better than I ever could. She danced with me in the rain at music festivals. She was a master in the Dark Art of Curing Hangovers, and the morning after said music festivals would deliver kebabs, salty hot chips, freshly fried nuggets or bowls of creamy carbonara to my bedside. Night after night, our bedrooms were lit up by the glow of iPhones and the rapid streams of texts and emojis and screenshots accompanied with nothing but '!!!!!!!!!!' or '???????' or '.........'.

We were extensions of each other. We were each other's limbs until the obstacle course of our twenties proved we were only slowing each other down.

~

Severing a limb. That's the feeling of breaking up with your best friend. This person has been in your life for a long time. You know the inside of her car like Gretchen Wieners' lines from *Mean Girls*. You've memorised her cousins' names, her preferred concealer brand and shade, the minor changes she requests when ordering the local cafe's halloumi fritters. She's the one who perfectly curated all those replies to that ludicrously tall guy from work. She got you your fake ID when you were sixteen and bailed you out when your dad found it in your wallet, too. She has been there since what feels like forever, riding the waves of teenage angst and awkwardness by your side, squeezing your hand a little tighter whenever you lost your footing.

But, over time, she has also become the one who makes you feel lonely. It wasn't a standalone event that did it; her breadcrumbs just led you to an uncomfortable truth. As you grew older and stepped further away from the teenage years that fused you together, her true self emerged, and you're not sure if you like that person so much anymore. You suspect that maybe she doesn't feel so crash hot about you, either.

Like the time you go out clubbing together, and she organises for a guy to pick the two of you up from the city. The guy needs to collect something from his mate's place on the way back to yours, she tells you. Only, when he parks in the foreign driveway, she follows him inside, and insists they'll be back in just a second. Almost half an hour later, it will dawn on you that she's left you in a stranger's car, in another stranger's driveway, in the middle of winter. You're wearing nothing but a Kookai mini-dress, because you're twenty and – despite your mother's begging – too stupid to dress for the weather just yet. Your phone has now died, too. Not that it matters, because she didn't respond to your first four texts and calls anyway. You'll go up to the strange house and try to open the door, but it's locked, so you return to the car. When she comes to collect you three hours later, and hears your chattering teeth, she'll insist she developed some sort of amnesia – you see, he's really hot and she forgot you existed. *It's not that bad,* she writes in a text that you receive when you open your front door and realise there's no time to sleep because it's 7.30 am and therefore time to start getting ready for your retail job. *You're just being dramatic.*

Or the time she started fooling around with one of your friends despite knowing he has a long-term girlfriend – a girlfriend she's met on about a dozen occasions. You know this because you were there. All twelve times. You really like the girlfriend, actually. She's a sweet girl who has no fucking idea that your best friend is meeting up with her boyfriend in secret when he should be at football training. At first, you'll try to ignore what's happening and sever ties with just the dickhead guy. You'll instruct yourself to believe her when she tells you it was stupid, that she regrets it. But then you're out on a Saturday night and she's licking his teeth and biting his lips when the girlfriend is at the bar buying drinks. Your friend is delighting in their sick and twisted game of cat and mouse. The worst part comes when she tells you she doesn't even really like him. What she likes is the attention. The thrill is too titillating to stop.

The friendship glitter is still there but it's fading. You continue to giggle at stupid movies, to go on Macca's runs to satisfy late-night McFlurry cravings. The friendship just doesn't feel so ... warm anymore. There's frostiness. You feel it in the spaces of quiet, the ones you now clamber to fill. You feel it in the ever-so-lightly-forced laughter that has replaced the deep belly chuckles.

You wonder if she feels it, too.

You begin to feel uncomfortable with how she speaks to baristas at cafes, to your sisters, your mum, and, sometimes, you. You see her texts and don't feel like replying quickly – or, sometimes, even replying at all. She points out that your skin has been looking pretty dodgy lately, and maybe you should stop wearing eyeshadow, because it highlights the constellation of acne currently sprawling across your cheeks. You point out that she still owes you $12 for that coffee and croissant last Thursday.

She tells you that you sound really stuck up and should consider an attitude adjustment. You tell her you'd rather be stuck up than someone who sleeps with other people's boyfriends. She asks you to name the last time you checked in with her to see how she's doing – how she's *really* doing – and you'll realise you haven't done that in a very long time. She might be someone else's other woman, but at least she bothers to ask you how you are.

Soon it feels like every week, every day, you're testing each other's boundaries of what constitutes a good friend and what defines a bad one. No new oxygen is flowing into the friendship anymore. Something's died, here, and it died some time ago. The limb is gangrenous and you don't want to talk about a cure. What you want is to amputate.

There's a lot of chatter about relationship deal-breakers when the relationship in question is romantic. *Look for the red flags!* we tell each other. *Oh, and did we mention the yellow ones? Here! There are squiggeldy-million books and eleventy-hundred movies to tell you precisely what you don't want.*

RELATIONSHIP DEAL-BREAKERS

- Doesn't want kids!

- Is untrustworthy!

- Lacks drive and ambition!

- Is allergic to dogs!

- Considers re-watching the second season of *Fleabag* every three months a 'waste of time'!

But what about the deal-breakers for platonic love?

We don't hear so much about these. Instead, we have shows like *The Bold Type*, replete with the most concrete of bonds: invincible, soulful, brilliant friendships that thrive on cocktails and curious (read: really quite awful) outfits.

Maybe that's why I entered my twenties with a list of what I wanted in a boyfriend (clever, witty, kind, nurturing) and what I didn't (selfish, sexist, condescending) but with absolutely nothing to guide my friendships. My friends just *were*. I got along with them most of the time and that was enough.

But if screaming at each other in a maxi taxi while the poor driver tries to glean your home address between snivels teaches you anything, it's that it helps to define precisely what your friendship deal-breakers are. You should have a list and, in testing times, you should check it. Check it twice! Kind of like Santa. Only, this doesn't involve presents, unless you consider getting rid of toxic friends a present (which you absolutely should, by the way).

Here's my list.

FRIENDSHIP DEAL-BREAKERS

- Has a moral and ethical belief system that greatly conflicts with my own.

- Isn't happy for me when I achieve something.

- Responds to my happiness with negativity.

- Makes me feel small.

- Makes me recite her rather ridiculous order of a three-quarter half-strength very hot almond milk latte when it's my turn to grab coffee. (Less important. Also a subtle jab at Zara, who either wants her coffee to be three-quarters full or extra strong but never both at once.)

Of course, there is also a chance that in your twenties, friends will fall away not because you become different people, but because it's easy to lose each other in the noise.

Moving through your twenties will expose you to several unfortunate realities.

First of all, if you're over the age of twenty-five, your chance to date Leo DiCaprio has well and truly expired. Sorry.

The second? You'll probably start seeing your friends less and less. Those Saturday nights out clubbing will be replaced by Sunday brunch every fortnight, then every three weeks. Sometimes you will share Google Calendars and realise there are no overlapping windows of free time for a month and the only way to stay on the same page with what *Married at First Sight* contestant is The Worst is via weekly phone calls while you rid your pantry of old, sprouty, Grade-Six-science-experiment-worthy potatoes.

Friendships easily disintegrate when you forget to make those calls. Which you will, by the way. For some people. But you'll also notice that there are others – two or three, if you're lucky – that you never forget to call. Because no matter what's happening, they're bobbing in your mind, moored to you and all of this commotion, an anchor in the sea of change.

At nineteen, I didn't realise how truly rare good friends are; that finding someone who loves you when you sob into their new silk pillowcase just as much as they do when you yell 'MY SHOUT' over the DJ music is like stumbling upon a unicorn. It took moving into full-time work and meeting my first real friend since high school – Zara – to be reminded of how wonderful it is to find a new mate, to get to know them and to keep them, even when things get tricky and tense.

Some of my friendships are done, gone for good. But as much as it hurt to let them go, those break-ups clarified what I do and don't want from my friendships, and the kind of friend I want to be. They made me want to hold on to who is left with all my might. They made me want to channel as much energy as I can muster into the women I love and who love me back, because it's scarily easy to lose each other in the chasm.

I lost a best friend, and now we're nothing to each other. Only, not really. Because her shadow will always be there. I still know her phone number off by heart. She'll always be the person who could tell when I was grumpy about something based purely on the arch of my eyebrows. The one I called to tell the news of my life – happy and sad and in between.

Losing her sketched out the ebbs and flows that define this decade of confusion; it showed me that under the pressure of finding careers, love, wellbeing, adventures, *ourselves*, we fuck up. We act in ways we didn't think we were capable of, and sometimes our transgressions are a little more serious than gladiator sandals and fuckboys named Jack.

It also taught me in the harshest possible way that there's always room to be a better, more patient, more forgiving friend – not the one who judges from the sidelines. It taught me to cherish those special moments spent eating chicken carbonara by the bowlful and giving each other manicures under the blue light of a cheap, at-home nail kit, because now those memories are all that's left. The heartbreak showed me that sometimes, in order to grow, you need to let people go.

It was the right decision, to end the friendship. We had become different people. We weren't what the other needed anymore. But part of me will always hope that maybe one day we'll see each other across a bar, at the supermarket, or the gym, and grin – ready to catch up on everything that's happened in the space between.

The space between me and my best friend

I remember the day my best friend Sam told me she had booked her flights to move far, far away. It was a weekday, perhaps a Monday morning, and we were walking (read: dawdling) from my house to our local cafe of choice. Her overly well-behaved dog Gizmo loitered quietly at our ankles. In the space between ordering our coffees and having them in our hands, she turned to me, almost nonchalantly, and grinned.

'So, I've booked!' she said.

She was going to London and she was leaving in six months.

I'm not sure why surprise was my first emotion, for this certainly wasn't the first time Sam had told me of her plans. They had been bubbling below the surface and sneaking into our conversations for the better part of a year by this point, her musings about a new life in London rearing their head every time a conversation about our futures popped up.

It's just that for all she spoke, I still didn't believe her. We were twenty-two, life was simple and things felt cosy. It ain't broke, I thought, so why fix it? Our social lives were active, our university degrees under our belts, our long-term boyfriends keeping us company.

I met Sammy when we were twelve, and when I say I 'met' Sammy when we were twelve, I mean I first met Sammy virtually when she assaulted my parents' email inbox with lively pre-teen messages after my best friend from primary school, Georgia, put us in touch. We would be going to the same high school, and so Sam thought it was appropriate (and of utmost importance) that we become penpals in the months leading up to school starting. It was, I came to learn, characteristic of a Sam I'd quickly grow to love: she was never short of an overfriendly introduction. She loved dogs (too much), looked much cooler than she really was (she wasn't cool at all) and was invariably laughing louder than anyone else in the room. At twelve, alongside my other best friend Emily, Sam became a firm fixture in my life.

By the time we turned twenty-two, we were enveloped by an incredible sense of stability. She wasn't going anywhere, I promised myself. For over ten years, she hadn't gone anywhere. Why would she go now? Why would she go at all?

It turns out she *was* going somewhere, and she was going somewhere soon. London was calling, and the world suddenly felt larger than it ever had before. She had a job, a home and a plan. She had flights. She was ready to go. I acutely remember having a kind of existential crisis in the ensuing six months about over-committing to someone who was just about to leave me. It was dramatic, but so am I, and what's the point of being twenty-two if not to be hyperbolic about the worries you hold dear?

It's a funny thing, I realised at the time, the kind of grief you feel for a loss that isn't one. She was always going to be a phone call away, never more than a message. I would visit her and she me and we were steadfast in our commitment to communication. *You must tell me if your coffee order changes*, we both promised, *or if you're still thinking about getting that rogue haircut or if things start to overwhelm you to the point where your hold on the world begins to strain.*

There I was at just twenty-two, wondering whether the intensity of our friendship was the biggest blessing or the deepest curse. Because with strong bonds come keen losses. And she was moving far, far away. At the time, I made the joke that I would feel her loss as much as I'd feel the loss of my then-boyfriend moving away, so reliant was I on her presence, her kindness, her silliness and her laugh.

She'd be over there, I'd be over here. How does friendship work when geography rears its great, big, expansive head? Of course, I knew then – and know even more so now – the simple answer is that it just does. It works because the bond we had meticulously built was a bond that defied distance. The bond we had created was the kind that allowed us – and continues to allow us – to roam free for a little while, before eventually making our way back together.

It's just that in that moment, standing coffee-less in the cafe as we watched Gizmo wait patiently by the kerb, the most inflexible, fearful, lazy part of me wasn't so keen to test it out. I was thick in that period of early adulthood where love isn't yet the be-all and end-all and family is a little further away, and had found it was my friendships that were defining my identity. My friends were the walls I leant on, the counsel I relied on, the ones I saw myself in. On their shiny, good, blindingly beautiful days, my friendships have kept me treading water when my arms grew tired. It's the gaggle of girlfriends around me who have carried me through the times I couldn't walk alone, their intricate understanding of our shared experience keeping me warm with their words or their visits or their jokes.

Distance, geography and funky time zones weren't going to change that. I imagined we would adjust and bend and work with what we had. I imagined it to be this way, because I imagine there aren't many people in this world today who don't have at least someone they love who's on the other side of it.

It was a suffocatingly warm day in January when Sam got on that plane, alone, to dark, drizzly London. I remember getting in the car after seeing her off and bursting into tears. I wondered how my waking hours would work when she was sleeping through them, how my weekends would function when my 'yes person' wasn't around. I remember imagining the day she moved home, and I remember wondering if we would ever be as close again.

People have since asked me, in the nearly three years since she left, how we have managed to hold it all together. How, despite living in different time zones and different cities, through romantic-relationship breakdowns and romantic-relationship reunions, she's still one of the closest people in my life. How we are closer today than maybe we have ever been.

In those moments I've always laughed, shrugged and hypothesised it's because we always make time for each other. I've never quite told them the minutiae of it all, of the effort it takes to have someone's back when you're not even there to physically hold it. Of the tiny, almost-inconsequential actions that are the bedrock of the relationship we share.

It is her calling me every day at the same time for two weeks after I ended a long-term relationship, pretending to check in about my day when I knew in reality she was checking in on my mind.

It's me remembering the names of every person she is working with, of noting down the times of her ever-changing work shifts, of knowing which days are stressful and which ones aren't.

It's her calling every few days on her morning commute to

work, making sure to always check in, even if it's to chat about nothing much at all.

It's me remembering to call the week the window in her room wouldn't close so her nights were noisy, and find out was she sleeping better now?

It's her asking so many consecutive questions about my life that I get off the phone and realise I just spent three quarters of an hour talking about myself.

It's feeling like there's not a story I could burden her with, not an issue I could complain about too much, no level of good news that would inspire jealousy.

It's having markedly different personalities but almost mirroring values, of being in periods with considerably different priorities but equal respect for each other's. It's knowing that the value of our friendship now comes with perspective: we're no longer so entwined in each other's lives that our advice is muddied with bias.

The other thing I never told those people who wondered how we kept our friendship burning bright beyond borders was that navigating a friendship that lives almost exclusively on WhatsApp is not without its difficulties. For all the effort I go to in understanding the details of her life, my lack of physical presence in Sammy's space means there are some things I can never glean, parts of her world I will never know and new relationships I won't ever be a part of.

Her local cafe or restaurant won't ever be mine, her commute not one I recognise. Her new friendships are forged through stories I hear but don't quite understand, over an intimacy that comes from the common experience of living far from home that I will never, ever share. Yes, our relationship is strong, and yes, I love her dearly but no, I don't think a long-distance friendship can exist without tiny, fleeting flashes of envy. The reality is Sammy and I haven't walked in sync for every moment she has lived over there, because of course, the dynamic shifts and changes and takes on a new life.

Friendships are generally a little bit magical, but our ability to keep them strong is not magic. I feel desperately lucky to have found her, but I do not feel luck has played a part in keeping us together. A strong bond isn't destined to endure everything. Not all friendships survive the kind of gaping geographical distance that comes with a friend moving thousands of kilometres away. Truthfully, not all friendships survive the gaping distance that comes not from geography, but maturity.

Nothing in our design or our future says Sam and I are destined to be friends forever. Nothing in the make-up of our relationship says that what we have will withstand every hurdle. But, I know we will because our relationship is strong, and our desire to work at it is stronger. Our friendship is firm, and the effort we put into keeping it stitched together is firmer.

When I was younger and I heard people talk about long-distance friendships, they talked about them in the context of a reunion, of two friends coming back together. In the context of time having passed and nothing having changed. But what about navigating long-distance friendships in real time as they transpire? What about the space between leaving and coming home? There's no guide to making them work, no rulebook on how to ensure the friendship defies physical separation and new work, new friends and new love.

When people ask about our friendship now, I can tell them it works because we never pushed pause. We're not on sabbatical, we're not taking a break, we're not making the assumption that we will simply pick things up the minute she moves home. I can tell them the flame of our friendship is burning as bright with space as it did without it. That it was forever our intention to keep it alight.

I can tell them distance isn't a death wish.

The Sammy who got on a plane that blazing summer day in Melbourne hadn't so much as visited London in her life, hadn't yet worked a day in her chosen career and needed a year to come full circle in deciding what she wanted in love.

The Zara who Sammy left that afternoon hadn't started a podcast, hadn't yet sorted out what she wanted from her career or her relationships and was yet to learn the value of cutting ties with the things that no longer served her.

I wish I could travel back to that Hampton cafe and tell the younger version of me that Sammy would leave and everything would be fine. That Sammy would leave, and she'd still be my rock. That Sammy would leave, but that I would always find her: in her new home, or in new corners of the globe we would visit together, or even at the end of a phone line.

That Sammy would leave, and it would likely be the best thing that happened to either of us, because it meant we would see different worlds, do different things, grow up in different ways and still hold tight to the rope that had bound us since the moment her first email hit my parents' inbox.

That Sammy would leave, and maybe one day I would leave to go somewhere, too, but that no amount of travel or moving or jobs or love or heartbreak would separate us. That we would make sure nothing, not even walls of water, time zones or distance, would dint the bond we'd built. That the space between us would always be filled with each other.

A letter to my toxic friend

To my toxic friend,

I write this to you from my new home, the one you have not visited yet. It's not that you're banned from coming, it's just, well . . . I've been quietly putting my walls up. There's a little more distance between us right now, but I think you can feel that, can't you? You can feel me pulling away.

There's so much I want to tell you. There have been times I've wanted to sit you down and talk you through why I'm going quiet, and other times when I've wanted to pull out a notepad and write down all the reasons I need to spend less time with you.

I feel nervous. About this, and around you. I get nervous that I'll do something you don't like or say something that will offend you. I tiptoe around you: around your moods, your unpredictability and your propensity to get angry at me for the smallest of indiscretions.

When I told you about my promotion, you asked why I had told other friends first. When I fell in love with my boyfriend, you said I wasn't there for you anymore. When I got approved for my first apartment, you took the opportunity to tell me why renting was 'dead money'.

I am tired of not being able to tell you when good things happen; when I feel happy or when small windfalls of success come my way. I don't appreciate the inference that by design of being fulfilled in my relationship and career, I am getting too big for my boots. I am tired of only being able to share the bad times, the negativity, my insecurities.

I am sick of feeling like you want me to be smaller, like you get kicks out of cutting me down.

I know things may not be going well for you right now. I know that, I really do. I know things worry you and make you sad, I know the world feels hard and harsh and too big, sometimes.

I know you are struggling.

But I need to be honest here. I am wracked by the guilt of our friendship. Consumed by it, even. I lose sleep over not being around enough for you, not doing enough for you, not *being* enough for you. Sometimes I wonder what it would take to appease you, to make you happy. I wonder if there will ever be a time when I feel like my feet aren't chronically making missteps, or when my priorities are perfectly in line with your own.

I am writing to tell you that, despite all the guilt I feel, I cannot continue this friendship in its current form. I feel bruised by your passive-aggressive comments, your demand for me to always be there. I am exhausted by your games, the need to constantly read your mind and the expectation that I should absorb your unhappiness whenever you need to unload.

So, if you're wondering why I'm not around as much, why I'm not pinging your phone with messages and memes the second you go cold on me, it's because this friendship has begun to deplete me. I need to take some time to recalibrate with people who make me feel full again.

I care about you deeply. That will never change.

But for now, I need to prioritise the friendships that feel equal and joyful – not the ones that make me feel like I'm failing a test I didn't even know I was taking. Maybe one day we will find our way back to each other, and tell each other everything that happened in between. I hope you find friendships that fulfil you and soothe you and make you feel seen. We all deserve that, I think.

Love,

Me x

The space between
my parents

– MICHELLE –

There's an unspoken camaraderie between those who come from broken families.

You know the ones. The families who never quite recovered from the split, the ones who are still nursing cuts and bruises all these years later. The families with parents who only communicate with each other through their children or their lawyers. The families who look at other separated parents who made it work – who became friends, despite everything – and feel their hearts contort.

As adults, most of us try to downplay the impact of our parents' splits. I mean, c'mon! We're all *adults* now, and in the greater scheme of things (cancer, drug dependency, criminal charges, death, waking up to find Instagram is down again) our parents deciding to call it quits is hardly earth-shattering. We rattle off statistics to try to make the punch to the face feel more like a nudge to the ribs. *Almost half of all marriages end in divorce!* we say. Also, *Humans are living longer now, and we can't expect people to stay together for their entire lives anymore.* We rationalise and compartmentalise and intellectualise and joke, but having your family fall apart feels a lot like grief.

The decline of my parents' marriage was cataclysmic. It feels dramatic admitting that five years later, but that's precisely what it was. It doesn't matter how common it is, how utterly predictable it is – it still scars the same. You can smell the emotional trauma, that same pain and confusion, on some of the people around you. There's a gravitational pull towards unlikely acquaintances, simply because their scars look an awful lot like yours.

The first phone call I made through heaves and sobs wasn't to anyone in my inner circle; it was to a distant friend from high school who knew how it felt to be blindsided by her parents, how it felt to have the fabric of your life torn in two without explanation. Hey, Sandra! Please, tell me: was it an affair, a gambling problem, a mid-life crisis, or five years of blink-and-you-miss-them little red flags that did it for your parents?

Were you told on a couch? At the dining table? In your bedroom?

Did you worry about taking sides?

What did you learn that you really didn't want to?

How does it feel to be your parents' confidant, as well as their child?

The call only lasted five or six minutes, and the splutters that interrupted every word didn't allow her to offer all that much, but I found solace in that phone call months after I hung up. Because if you know what it's like, you get it. You get the pressure, the anger, the guilt, the befuddlement that comes with seeing two people you love with all your heart go to war. You get the sadness that comes with seeing your parents at their lowest, their angriest, their pettiest. You too feel the sideline anxiety that comes with engagement parties and funerals, because you know that as much as you should be focusing on the event itself, your parents are going to see each other again and there's no way of knowing how that will go. You've grown a little tired of echoing the news of your life events twice – in the exact same way – because there is no shared space now. No, now there are two kitchen tables, two restaurants, two Christmases.

And then there's you.

You, the child who bounces between them, trying desperately to share yourself equally so that feelings are not hurt and allegiances are not drawn.

It was the day after my friend Emily's twenty-first birthday party when everything went wrong. A fight erupted over something ambiguous and Dad was gone. When my mum told my siblings and me that she thought he was leaving their marriage, we chuckled in disbelief. The thought of Dad leaving Mum seemed so far-fetched, so ridiculous that we didn't even entertain the possibility. But Mum was right.

It took a month for him to move out of my parents' bed and onto the couch, then into a hotel, and finally into an apartment five minutes away. When he told us all of his decision – that yes, this was it, he was leaving Mum – it was almost midnight on a Friday. There we sat, all six of us, around the coffee table that had been a fixture of our lives for so long, but instead of chatting about netball games, university classes or school results, we discussed Dad moving out. When everything that could be said had been said, I grabbed a packet of potato chips and ate them with my sisters and mum upstairs. I slept in Mum's bed that night. I didn't return to my own for two weeks.

Over the next few months, each day started with the upsetting reminder that things were different. Things were broken. The mood in our house had shifted. My mum cried on the phone to the telephone company when she couldn't pay the bill because her name wasn't on the account. Lights were always on because someone was always awake. I watched Netflix late into the night because for the first time in my life, I struggled to sleep. When I finally drifted off around three or four am, I would grind my teeth so badly I couldn't open my jaw properly when I woke for uni.

I'd always considered myself a perceptive person, and yet I really, truly didn't see it coming. That dissonance made me question everything I thought I knew about myself. Could I really be emotionally intelligent if I didn't notice my own parents' marriage fraying? I was *right there*. I had lived with them for twenty-one years and yet my perception of my own life and the people within it was so at odds with reality. What else had I missed? What else was fake? What else was weaker than it looked from the outside?

It felt like we'd been living in front of a trick mirror and now the lights had been flicked on to reveal that our perfect life had been disintegrating behind the two-way glass the whole time. With every week that passed, the chasm between perception and reality widened. Even now, I look back at family holiday photos, all sparkly grins and shiny faces, and can't quite remember what it was like before everything collapsed.

I fought with Dad because I didn't know how else to channel my anger. I glared at him over dinners at my grandparents' house. I sent him curt emails and text messages. I snapped at him for not trying harder. I bubbled with fury whenever I heard Mum crying in her bedroom. I cried at cafes when he asked how we were doing.

I became obsessed with retracing the past. My siblings and I would sift through the years – childhood, adolescence, adulthood – with forensic interest, holding up the most innocuous moments and rotating them in search of answers.

'Is this where it all fell apart?' we would ask each other, psychoanalysing our parents. Didn't they do something really romantic for their anniversary last year? When was their last fight? Their last date? Their last kiss?

We asked lots of questions. We got lots of answers.

That's the thing about your parents splitting when you're twenty-one and not eleven: you're told the things that little kids are shielded from. You're savvy enough to determine the ins and outs of what's going on and you're trusted to cope with the truth. Only, you're too young and dumb to actually do anything helpful with it, so you spend your nights crying in nightclub bathrooms to strangers about your parents' relationship breakdown.

You're still their child, but there's a blurring of the lines. You're the only one who can truly help make sense of what happened – what went wrong, and why – because, well, you were there. That level of insight can't be replicated in a family friend. It belongs only in the minds of whoever lived through it. You know too much – far too much to ever go back to how things were. You also can't really offer any morsels of wisdom, because, as much as you try to be the purveyor of sage advice, your relationship experience is nothing more than a trail of failed situationships and Tinder matches that never eventuated in dates.

In the darkest times of our parents' marriage breakdown, my siblings and I functioned more as their friends than we did their children. We were told the details of what had chipped away at their marriage over the years. We were leant on for advice and insights because it was considered better to keep things in the family than to share things externally.

Sometimes – often – we felt like the gatekeepers of all the

top-secret information, the ones left to decide who would tell one parent about the other's new partner. The adults, really.

I was happy that I could be the lighthouse for my parents' split, but I was also sad. I'm *still* sad. Part of me still feels like my childhood has slipped away; that the ink of my little memories has run, bleeding into the grown-up memories, distorting the colour and shape of everything that once felt simple.

In the rubble of my parents' marriage, it felt like the six of us were meeting each other – with all of our quirks, flaws and idiosyncrasies – for the very first time.

I've grown closer to my parents since they separated; our conversations are richer and infused with intense honesty. Sometimes, I wonder if they had stayed together, would I have ever had the chance to know them and love them as individuals, in the way I have after their split?

Now I retreat to Mum's place at every chance I get to watch footy and drink tea. We talk about how my girlfriends are, how my boyfriend Mitch is going at work, what I think about the latest political story to seize the news cycle, or why Damien Hardwick dropped Richmond's second-best forward for Friday night's game. Mum is one of the warmest, kindest, most eloquent people you could ever meet. She speaks with conviction and intelligence. I'm the writer and yet I'm sure I'll never be able to match her vocabulary. She's passionate and dedicated to her career as a speech pathologist. She finds intense joy in helping people. She makes the best goddamn meatballs you'll ever taste in your life. She's the only person I know who calls me 'Shelly' and I like it that way. She gives the best hugs. She radiates love.

Saturday morning brunches with Dad are often the highlight of my week. We split a ham and cheese toastie and toss around big social questions – like the complexities of the word 'progressive', or the shortcomings of Twitter's echo chambers. He is the best critical thinker I know. He makes me erupt in laughter one second and think deeply about my place in the world the next. He's a fantastic listener. He gives such wise advice. I wish everyone could spend just an hour with him, because I don't think there's a person on this planet who wouldn't benefit from a deep and meaningful chat with my dad over a latte. He calls me 'Michy' and responds to my texts with a million colourful emojis. He makes a mean curry, even though he'll always find something that isn't quite right when he eats it. His eyes fill with tears when he talks about how much he loves his kids. My eyes fill with tears when I think of just how much he means to me.

My siblings and I have an unbreakable bond. We were always tight-knit but now we are fused together like steel rods. We fill the space between our parents; we're stronger than I ever thought possible. Our parents' split taught us lots about romantic relationships. It taught us the importance of being honest; that having a fight in the moment is always better than bottling it up. It taught us to pursue our passions, because feeling fulfilled outside of a relationship is crucial if you want to feel fulfilled within one. It taught us that you need to talk with candour as often as possible, especially when it feels awkward. It taught us to check in with our partners every now and then to compare notes on how things are travelling. It taught us that more than anything, literally anything, you need to be able to have fun together. You need to be able to play-fight and giggle and rib each other when the moment calls for it.

I am terrified that my relationship will end like my parents'. If their love could end so brutally, what's to say mine will be any different? But I know now that love moves and changes. It is a stupefying, shape-shifting thing. I also know that even if you do all the right things to protect it, the love might still move on some day, because that's life and life can be shitty. Maybe you'll lose the love you have now. Maybe I will, too. But the pain and hurt that pulls you apart doesn't make the love not worth it. That person you gave your heart to handed you some things in return: lessons, experiences, wisdom. That stuff doesn't die. It guides you towards a better, brighter love. And so maybe you don't need to speak to each other anymore. Maybe you don't need to be in each other's lives at all. That's okay. These things don't have to be straight-forward. But the love was there, and it was real.

And when it was good? It was brilliant.

The separation was neither my mum's nor my dad's fault. Both were grief-stricken over what had happened – for different reasons, of course, but I've come to learn that doesn't matter. The heartbreak of choosing to break up a family and move away from your kids is no gentler than the heartbreak of having your soul-mate tell you they don't love you anymore. It might be different, but that doesn't make it any easier. Heartbreak is heartbreak.

It's clear that the shape of my family will never be the same. I've grown to accept that some cuts will never heal. I still ache for that family unit, that team we used to be. I ache for it around Christmas, and when there's particularly exciting news that one of us wants to share. I ache for it on my birthday, when I'd really prefer to blow out the candles on one cake, not two. I ache to be in a room – any room – with both my mum and my dad without feeling like they are two magnets repelling each other into separate corners.

But I'm okay. Really. I still have my parents. They are clever, witty, wonderful human beings. They are my friends. I love them with all my heart. No matter how broken and lost their love for each other is, it's still spinning magic, lighting up my world with my sisters, my brother, my mum, my dad, and all the memories we've created along the way.

And I've grown to learn that's enough.

LOVE

The downsides and upsides
of having a sister

DOWNSIDES	UPSIDES
She will steal your shit and lie to you about it.	You can steal her shit and lie to her about it.
Her. Moods.	She's one of the only people in the world who can handle your moods, and settle them (and you) when the world feels too much.
She can be really fucking melodramatic.	She doesn't point out when your stories have a little bit of . . . mayonnaise . . . on them.
She gives brutal, borderline scathing life advice.	You can trust that she'll tell you things exactly as they are, because she knows you can handle it when it's coming from her.
She does not care for your sensitivities.	She can cut through your shit with a machete.
She will literally always tell you what to do.	She's usually really fucking bang-on about how you should live your life.
She's annoyingly competitive.	She pushes you to do better and be better.
She pushes your buttons more than anyone you know.	She knows you better than you know yourself.
You have the most explosive arguments known to mankind.	Literally nothing (caveat: maybe murder) could destroy your bond.
She has no issue cutting you down to size.	She's the only reason your head isn't high in the clouds.

DOWNSIDES	UPSIDES
If she's younger than you, she will copy every single thing you do.	If she's younger than you, you're someone's role model. She would clone you and be you if she could.
If she's older than you, she will always be your parents' favourite.	If she's older than you, she'll be the parent figure you crave when your mum and dad can't be there.
She'll save the worst parts of her personality just for you.	You'll see her at her lowest, but also her brightest and happiest too.
She might just be the most judgemental person in the entire world.	You have someone to vent all of your shameful, judgemental crap to, because you're certain she's thinking the exact same thing.
You will be the butt of every single one of her jokes.	You will laugh more hysterically with her than anyone else.
She'll tell you whenever she hates your friends.	She's the most accurate Toxic Human detector going around, and can spot a crappy friend approximately eleven years before you do.
You don't need to ask if she hates your new boyfriend. It's all over her face.	You don't even need words to communicate about the things that matter. You need one look to know what the other is thinking.
Sorry, but she's needy as fuck.	If something happens, you have someone to spam with phone calls and texts. She's your rock, you're hers, and you need each other when life gets rocky.
She definitely bitches about you to your mum.	She's great to have a bitch about the extended family with.
Half the stuff she says is nonsensical.	You only ever truly embrace your weird side when you're together.
She sings terribly and often. (Did we mention terribly?)	There's absolutely nothing that compares to car rides together, belting out 'Umbrella' by Rihanna.
Wherever you go, she's there.	And you wouldn't have it any other way. Despite everything, you're soulmates.

The space between being an adult and my parents' child

— ZARA —

I was seventeen and hiding out in my room when my dad came knocking on my door. It was a Saturday afternoon and he asked me to come downstairs.

'Could we chat?'

For no substantial reason at all, or perhaps just because I was seventeen, sullen and deliberately difficult, I told him that no, we couldn't. I was busy!

He pushed a little more.

'All the others are downstairs. I need you down there, too.'

I swapped out my excuses for something I thought would stick this time. I was actually developing stomach cramps and couldn't move from bed. Could we have that chat later?

'I need you downstairs and I need you down there now.'

Clutching my stomach to back my own lie, I trudged downstairs to where my two brothers, sister and mum were all congregated around a couple of red three-person couches. My parents, never ones to dwell on bad news, were gentle in their delivery.

Dad had just been diagnosed with cancer and he would be fine and Mum and Dad were feeling fine but he would be taking some time off work for a while and, well, did we have any questions?

I remember distinctly surveying the room with two thoughts hovering in my mind: of course we didn't have any questions, because how can you have questions about something you know nothing about? Oh, and secondly: didn't my phantom stomach cramps look like a fucking parody now?

I don't remember things getting noisy or there being much commotion about the entire exchange. I remember very few words floating to the surface and not because my brothers and sister were revelling in the melodrama of deafening silence (truthfully, my three siblings are some of the least dramatic people I know). No words came to mind because nothing seemed appropriate. No words felt right because nothing made sense. Who would want to say anything thoughtless or unhelpful at a time when only the perfect response would suffice?

After no more than ten minutes, with an air of restlessness wrapping our home, we all just went back to our days. I remember twinges of guilt jabbing my conscience as I reopened my laptop, alone, in my bedroom. My thoughts felt scattered, like they were trying to land on ground that kept collapsing beneath them.

What's my role here?

I went back to studying and, that evening, to my best friend's eighteenth. On Monday, I went to school as I did every week, and sat through classes as I did every other weekday. My life looked like it always had; my weeks continued down their regular path.

What's my role here?

In holding it together, in resuming my day, in continuing to spin with the world, was I alleviating my dad's stress but refusing to acknowledge my own? Should I have stopped being such a child – should I have stopped being *his* child – for a second and offered him my damn shoulder when no words materialised in that first conversation? If I could go back in time and be part of that conversation again, would I be able to find words that would be of comfort? If I could go back in time, would the words be there at all?

It turned out, two years later and just months after he had fully recovered, I was given the opportunity to find out for sure.

'Could we chat?'

It was an otherwise unremarkable weeknight when my mum came knocking. She'd already rounded up my younger brother (my older siblings were out) and this time we sat upstairs in a clueless cluster across a beige, four-person couch.

Mum wasn't well and she would be fine and Mum and Dad were feeling fine but she would be taking some time off work for a while and, well, did we have any questions?

I remember surveying my mum's face this time, rather than the room. She was smiling her normal, sunny, cheek-reaching smile. It had a kind of tenacity to it. Trust my mother to be diagnosed with cancer and to play it down to such a degree that she forgot to actually tell us it was cancer.

I remember turning to my dad when she left the room and asking, specifically, what the deal was. It was breast cancer, he said, and it wasn't great but it wasn't terrible. (It took me three years to learn just how bad 'not great' actually is.) After no more than ten minutes, I went back to my room. That familiar feeling of guilt and disorientation took charge.

I was nineteen. In the eyes of the world and just about every system that exists to measure my maturity, I was an adult. I could drive and I could vote, I could drink and go to jail. But in that moment – and in many that would come after that – I still felt like a tiny, doe-eyed child.

What's my role here?

I hadn't yet been trained to be her protector or her shield; I didn't know which words made her mind settle or the kinds of things that brought her the most comfort. I had been by her side for nearly two decades, living in her corner and happily floating in her orbit. I knew she liked cups of chai tea and going for runs and walking aimlessly around shopping centres on her days off. And yet I didn't know what to say to my own mother in a time she was likely captured by fear.

What's my role here?

I want to be able to tell you our collective worlds shifted on their axes on the two days my parents told us their health had faltered. I want to be able to tell you I wrapped my arms around them and told them I loved them, that I would be there for them, that I would lend them my ears and my heart and both of my hands to hold, if that's what they needed. I want to be able to tell you I didn't just go back to my day and my work, that I didn't push ahead with the four-month overseas holiday my sister and I had already planned.

But onwards with my day I went, traversing from university to work to nightclubs as if my mother wasn't lying still at home, wishing the effects from this round of chemotherapy would finally wear off. My siblings and I pushed on, going through the motions and letting them pull us in their wake. There was no time to dwell, no space for self-pity. My parents had a remarkable ability to shield us from their pain; the cocoon that blanketed our family was made up of their hands and their hearts, their grit and their resolve. They did not let us play defender, they did not let it shake us, they did not let it consume us. And it didn't.

Their ill health was something we carried together, a trolley of

LOVE

small mishaps we pushed as one. It's just that as time went on, this doe-eyed, clueless teenager came to the brutal realisation that being a child wasn't a role I could own forever, that being *their* child wasn't a part I could play for eternity. That there would come a day when I would no longer be defined just as their child, but maybe as their equal, maybe as someone who should be holding them in the way they had always held me. Maybe it was finally time to find the words. As my thoughts wandered a little further, I began to think about the day I'd still be ambling across the world's terrain, and neither of them would be here to guide me.

~

I know that's the point of ageing.

I know we're meant to grow up and grow old. I know, rationally, that's how time works, but they don't really warn you about what happens when time forces that realisation on you, you know? When you realise that the people who have always held us and made us feel safe, home and whole aren't always going to be around to insulate us from the world. When you look at them and understand the world doesn't discriminate, and neither does its blows.

I sometimes wonder if the rise of 'adulting' jokes and memes – how we all pretend to be hopeless millennials without direction or skills or sophistication – is one great big nod to how disorientating it can be to find yourself no longer locked under the wing of someone who has always guided you. And how strange it is to realise that someday, the adults in our orbit will need our guidance as much as we have always needed theirs.

Absolutely, there's something to be said for how first-world – how *privileged* – it is to be swaddled for long enough to recognise when the blanket starts to slip. It's just that, whatever our relationship with our parents – whether it be fractured or full, complicated or clear – no one really talks about that moment where the exposing elements of adulthood make themselves known in a flurry, and you have no choice but to adapt or risk being left out in the cold.

When I asked Shameless Media's producer and community manager, Annabelle Lee, about her experience with a sick parent, she echoed many of the things I felt: the guilt of continuing to live your life as if nothing had changed when likely everything had changed for them, and the feeling of wanting to fix it all but having no inkling where to begin.

When Annabelle was a child she learned her beloved mother was suffering from schizophrenia. Last year, for the *Shameless* newsletter, she wrote about it for us:

> When I was around eight, my mum was first diagnosed with psychosis. Then schizophrenia, followed by delusional disorder. No, she didn't have all three, rather, her distrust in strangers meant a definite diagnosis was difficult to pinpoint by professionals. That same distrust led to medication flushed down the toilet, a marriage breakdown, and a super sunny adolescence! (Also, a deep-rooted tendency to express sarcasm during the worst of times. Try not to psychoanalyse me.)
>
> As the years progressed, I lost the parts of my mum I loved the most: her comforting words of encouragement, her melodic laughter, her maternal warmth. And eventually, I lost her trust, too. It was slow and agonising; an amalgamation of the heaviest pain, shame, and helplessness I'd ever felt. For so long, I struggled with what exactly this

was. In the moments I longed for the security of home, it felt like the woman who used to so confidently define the very concept of family was gone.

I asked her about what it feels like to realise, even as an adult, that your parents can't protect you from everything, particularly when they can't even protect themselves from their own mind.

'I know most parents would do almost anything for their kids, but almost anything isn't everything, that's just not possible. Realising that wasn't easy, but it also drew surprising clarity,' she says.

Annabelle's relationship with her mother possessed layers of complexity that mine didn't. For one, there's the stigma of mental illness that continues to be pervasive, despite much of the work we do collectively through the public discourse to change that. And secondly, Annabelle has to grapple with a changed relationship, a changed dynamic, not just a changed set of circumstances.

'Even to this day, I still feel like a kid,' she says. 'When Mum's condition was at its worst, with episode after episode of hers directed at me, I felt frustration and anger. I felt self-pity. I would cry and lock myself in my room, waiting for it all to blow over so she could be my mum again. I wanted Mum to fix it, even when I certainly knew she wasn't capable of doing so. Someone had to fix it; anyone but me.

'I used to blame her for not being able to see the world as I did, but I haven't done that in a while. Contrary to what I used to think, my mum isn't unbreakable. Actually, she's already been broken far too many times for it to be fair. And even though Mum would never ask for help, I know she needs me now like I always needed her.'

According to psychologist Sabina Read, there's something unique about coming into your twenties and landing on the realisation that, assuming we have a healthy relationship with our parents, there's more value to those bonds than we ever gave them credit for.

'When we are younger we think our parents will always be there, that they will have the answers, that they will look after us. We then go through a phase, probably our teenage years, where we think that parents know nothing and don't have the answers. And we're trying to pull away, which is really natural, to try to find our own individual selves. But this twentysomething age group, which is developmentally a new space, is one where you realise your parents do have a lot of wisdom and knowledge. They have a lot of love and support to give, and in most cases, you still really need that,' she says.

That idea of grief that Annabelle touched on – the kind you feel for a loss that isn't permanent or mortal, but for a relationship that no longer looks like it once did – is palpable in your twenties, Read says. If a parent is sick, we find ourselves consumed by a strange marriage of grief and guilt. We want so badly to help but we haven't yet been given the how-to manual.

'There are elements of grief that come with having an ill parent at that age: "You've been my mentor, you've been my guiding support, and now I need to do those things for you, but it's not a role I'm familiar with. I don't know how to do it." It's uncharted territory,' Read says. 'It's not that you don't have the tools. Sometimes you just simply can't change the circumstance. Depending on the severity of the situation, there are some things out of your control. I think there's a part of us that always continues to be the child. Those roles continue across the lifespan.'

For Annabelle, there's the prevailing sense that if our parents were infallible or invincible, then her mum would be better in a heartbeat. And, while it took her a little while to reconcile with that, she's settled on it now. Our parents aren't perfect, but of course, they are still *ours*. We are just the physical, walking products of their fears, hopes, bodies and minds.

'If I could zap away the schizophrenia, I know my mum would be there, exactly as the person I remember. I know how much she adores her children. I know she's an amazing mother. And I know that if she truly were invincible, she'd come back to us.'

It's been more than eight years since that first conversation with my dad on the red couch, and six since the one with my mum on the beige one. I still wonder whether, if you took me back to both of those couches, there would ever be a world in which I would have found the right words. I wonder, too, whether there would be a world in which anyone that age could, and would, have found the right words. Perhaps it only matters that I – that *we* – learn to find the words.

There's something funny about that line in the sand. You know, the line that exposes our parents' vulnerability. Yes, it marks a point where the dynamic changes, when it's not so much a one-way street and when you learn to be there for them as much as they are for you. But there's something lovely about a relationship that is a little more equal, where your bond is bolstered by being both a giver and a taker. Where you see them as whole and human, and not just as the people who raised you. Where you recognise the love you share as boundless and overwhelming, defined less by the roles you play and much more by the shrinking space and distance between you both.

29 things we wish we could have told ourselves on the final day of university

1. You are allowed to be stressed right now. This new period of your life is going to be daunting, but it's also going to be brilliant.

2. Some of those subjects were . . . an interesting use of your time and money. Lucky you won't realise the contemporary sociological theory class you bludged through will take three years to pay off until you read your first payslip.

3. Oh, and those subjects you failed? And the ones you opted out of after the census date cut-off? Yeah. We reeeeaaaaally wish you hadn't.

4. You don't have to pretend to be excited about finishing university if you don't know what's coming next. Uncertainty is scary.

5. And you don't need to tell everyone you 'might' go travelling, just to evade questions about job-hunting. Be honest. There is no shame in not knowing.

6. Finding a job on the career path you want is going to be tricky. It's not going to show up on your doorstep. Look for the windows that are cracked open slightly, not just the doors flung wide.

7. Learn how to network. And no, that doesn't mean getting a bunch of dorky business cards printed. It's as simple as introducing yourself with a smile. Remembering people's names. Being friendly. Asking questions.

8. That being said: people know when you're stalking them on LinkedIn. Beware.

9. Approach opportunities with enthusiasm!!! You can't control whether you're the most qualified!!! You can control whether you're the most enthusiastic!!!

10. Chill out on the emojis and exclamation marks in your emails (listicles are an exception to this rule). People can smell the nervousness through their computer screens. Less is best.

11. You are more than welcome to spend some time floating between jobs you might not love before working out what you want. There is no deadline or cut-off point when it comes to chasing your dreams. And no, you don't need to know exactly what that 'dream' is just yet. Things take time. Everyone is going at their own pace. You've got the rest of your life to figure out career stuff.

12. Stop looking for The Perfect Job. Look for a good, solid, dependable job. Don't stress about how it sounds or how it looks. Will it give you relevant experience? Will you meet new people? That's all you need for now.

13. Do your research before you rock up to a job interview. Do you know the history of the company? The name of your interviewer? The kind of role you're actually going for?

14. Accept that you're probably going to be on a semi-miserable salary for a year. As soon as that year is up, march into your

boss's office and prove why and how you're worth 10 per cent
more. Bring spreadsheets. And KPI reports.

15. Nothing will make you more valuable in the workplace than
    being the employee who takes initiative. Don't sit around
    twiddling your thumbs, waiting for someone to give you a task.
    Find a task and just do it.

16. Don't be afraid of appearing 'too keen'. That's not a thing.
    Tell people you want work. Make sure people can see you.

17. TAKE HOLIDAYS WHEN YOU'RE OWED THEM.

18. Same goes for lunchbreaks.

19. While we are here, take your sick leave when you're sick.
    Don't be a martyr. And if there's anything we have learned from
    2020, the rest of the office does not need your viral plague.

20. Oh and please, for the love of god, try to prepare your lunches
    at least one day a week. You can't afford Guzman y Gomez
    every single day. (Refer to number 14.)

21. Unpopular opinion: the structure and routine of full-time work
    is underrated. No matter the days you're working or the hour
    you're clocking on, there's something comforting about the
    rhythm of this new life.

22. Show up on time. Not two minutes late. It is the easiest way to
    make a good impression on the people who matter.

23. This is a bit grim, but . . . know that some HR departments are
    there to protect the company, not you.

24. Whatever you do, don't revel in the drama of the workplace.
    Being the office gossip will bring you plenty of headaches.

25. Acknowledge that you don't really know anything yet. That doesn't mean you shouldn't back yourself – you have some great things to offer – but it does mean listening to others and respecting their authority.

26. Walk that fine line between asking for what you want and knowing your place. For instance, your bosses don't need your input on how they should do their jobs. They absolutely should hear from you when you feel you deserve that big promotion.

27. In moments of self-doubt (they will come) emulate the confidence of a middle-aged, male real estate agent.

28. Fake. It. 'Til. You. Make. It.

29. Things will be okay. They will be so more than okay.

The space between what I thought my first job would be and how toxic it was

— ZARA —

I knew the media industry was going to be brutal. I was entering it at a time when jobs were scarce, morale was low and graduates were encouraged to take whatever work came their way in the name of experience. I knew I had to be scrappy, agile and agreeable. I knew I needed to do grunt work, to do weird work, to pick up the jobs no one else wanted. I was ready for that and I wanted that. I was desperate to be part of it all.

When I was twenty-one, after three years of random unpaid internships, I landed a job I had been desperate for. I was working as a content producer in women's media and was writing articles that boasted my own by-line. I was telling stories, playing with words, doing work I found fun and sugary on deadlines so tight that it felt exciting. This combination of naivety and gratitude meant that, in those early months, nothing could dull the rosiness with which I approached my work. It was a honeymoon period, but of a first-job kind: I was overenthusiastic, blinkered by my own employment status and awed by the perceived glamour of the work I was doing, that I dismissed the occasional tiny red flag as typical of a workplace that sometimes ran faster than its employees could walk.

Over the course of the next two years, though, the blinkers fell away and the rosiness clouded. The job took over my body and my psyche, my sleeping patterns and my social life. My working arrangements were constantly changing without my control or consultation, while the expectations for my performance were astronomical, despite having no resources at my disposal. If I wasn't a team player, if I wasn't ready and willing, I felt my job could disappear. I was young and, possessing an acute under-standing of the fickleness of the media industry, I did everything that was asked of me. Fear underpinned every sacrifice I made, every shift I said yes to, every task I took on.

I was working out of Melbourne in a satellite office some 878 kilo-metres from the company's head office in Sydney, where all the decision-makers were based. Looking back, the ease with which I adapted to almost unbelievable working conditions is terrifying. I have memories of our small office being home to rodents for the better part of five weeks. Five weeks with roaming rodents, including one particular day when I unknowingly worked eight hours with a dead one under my desk – which made me teary, but which the Sydney team seemed to find hilarious. Sure, I found it filthy, and sure, I demanded that things be fixed, but I grew used to the absurdity of my environment while waiting for something to finally be done about it. I grew used to not feeling secure or worthy of being taken seriously. I grew used to moving my work-station to the boardroom because the rodents hadn't found a way to invade that corner of the office yet.

I remember working on a weekend and feeling equal parts vulnerable and exposed because my colleagues and I had been tasked with running a news website without being given any legal training at all. I remember wondering every time I put my name to an article, or every time my editor published my work, if this was the story that would get us sued, or if this was the story that would sink my career before it had properly started.

Above all, I remember feeling like I didn't have support from HR, and the sense of betrayal that came with that. If I could not get a human resources department on my side, something designed to bridge the gap between employee and employer, what hope would I ever have?

With the wisdom of hindsight, I can see that it was a toxic workplace that bled into every part of my life: the highs were high, the lows were low and the time in between was a suction-like vortex of intense stress, quick turnarounds and an unrelenting concern that my job wouldn't exist in six months' time. My relationship with my job felt emotionally abusive; my mind oscillated between wondering if I was the problem or if the workplace itself was systemically troubled. Was I one of the millennial snowflakes derided by older generations? The entitled ones who asked the world of the world, who lacked both grit and drive and who couldn't hack the reality of the workforce?

It wasn't until I was two weeks out of that job that I realised I was never the problem. A fortnight after my final shift, I remember noting how physically light I felt. My shoulders weren't as tight, my mind not as scattered, and the knots that had entwined themselves in my stomach had uncurled. The nervous energy that was eating into every part of my body stopped biting, the rising tide of anxiety linked to my thoughts about work began easing. I was me again, coming back into my own to realise I'd never left myself to start with.

I knew my job wasn't good for me, but I'd never considered the fact that it was necessarily *bad* for me. Work was work, wasn't it? It didn't have to make your life better, it didn't have to make your world warmer, it just needed to not make things worse. Of course, the measure of a life worse off is a little hard to gauge when you're twenty-three and it's the only job you know. Or, to be blunt: it's hard to measure what's making your life worse when you've barely been an adult long enough to know what makes it better. I had been gaslighted into thinking my life was my job and my job was my life – because being in your twenties is about doing whatever it takes to get ahead, right?

The strangest thing about being completely absorbed by a toxic workplace is that sometimes you're in so deep you're not even sure what it is that is consuming you. I remember joking with many of the people I worked with about how our jobs felt emotionally abusive. The job felt unhealthy and yet, there was little to do but joke. Sometimes we would laugh, other days we would cry and then, when the giggles stopped or the tears dried up, we would turn back to our computers and get on with our work. But is it even fair to consider a workplace emotionally abusive? Is the term too much of a stretch?

'There is absolutely such thing as emotionally abusive workplaces,' organisational psychologist Michelle Pizer told me. 'It happens quite a bit, and the employee often asks me, "Am I making this up? Is it me or is it them? Am I overreacting?" I have seen some devastating consequences from people being part of emotionally abusive workplaces, resulting in months off work and serious mental health problems.'

In the same way they say that you can often only see a relationship was abusive with the power of hindsight, it wasn't until I left my job that I realised stress had overwhelmed my wellbeing. So, how can you work out whether a workplace is toxic if you're still in the thick of it?

'Symptoms might include feeling like it's unsafe to speak up, being too scared to ask for extra support, being given unreasonable work demands without the resources you need to perform your job or being asked to work unreasonable hours without an option of saying no,' Pizer says.

She concedes it can be hard to define 'unreasonable working hours' because that means something different from workplace to workplace, industry to industry. However, she says, it all comes down to why you are working the hours you are.

'In some cases, you can work crazy hours in a very supportive environment. But if you're scared and sitting on the edge of your seat all the time, and working these hours because you don't feel like you have an option or can keep your job otherwise, then that is intimidation. That's when you can tell it's gone too far.'

Since leaving that job, I've made it my mission to ask people about their experiences with workplaces that messed with their minds. Did they miss the signs, too? What would they change if they could go back?

In an interview Mich and I conducted with beauty editor and *Glow Journal* founder Gemma Watts last year, she spoke of how she found herself in a completely toxic workplace in her early twenties without knowing what she was embroiled in. At twenty-three, she realised she needed to get out.

'I worked as a fashion editor for five years and the business itself changed quite a lot in that time, to the point where I was very much ready to leave. So, that's what I did. On reflection, my friends, family and partner knew I was ready to leave about six months before I did,' she told us.

'It's very, very difficult to see a problem when you are that close to it. I've now been working for myself for upwards of two and a half years and the more time goes on, the more I look back and go, "No, you needed to leave much earlier than you did." But you just don't realise [that] at the time. There were situations that I was finding myself in that were absolutely not okay.'

Young people in the workplace are constantly told to be grateful for the work we're offered; that a good job is a privilege, not a right. And while that idea certainly rings true – a good job *is* a privilege – a safe, healthy workplace is not. The frequency with which we are told to be thankful for our own employment status creates a culture in which no one knows how to say no, or where saying no is akin to feeling like you will fall behind.

'You feel as though if you don't say yes to everything, someone else is going to come in and take that job. I was offered a huge opportunity interstate that I should have said no to, because looking back, the conditions were not okay. Not in the slightest,' Watts notes.

According to Anne Helen Petersen, author of the book *Can't Even: How Millennials Became the Burnout Generation*, it goes beyond the expectation that we should be grateful for any job we land on to the point where, if we find a job that suits us, we are made to feel that we should hold tight to it.

'I actually think we're past that point right now. Right after the global recession, there was a lot more rhetoric of gratefulness for any job, but now I think there's an understanding that you should find a job that's a good "fit", whatever that means,' she told me.

For some young people, the idea of a 'good fit' means finding a job that fits our – dare I say – personal brand. Does this job tie in neatly with my values? Could this job act as an extension of my personality? Is there an objective 'cool' factor or gravitas that comes with working for this company? Our fixation on the optics of what we do rather than the reality of our work means it's more likely we put up with a toxic workplace for the clout that comes with having a job that sounds better than it really is.

So, if you find yourself in a workplace that breeds toxicity: where do you go? Who do you turn to? Who can give you a sense check when all your senses feel skewed, manipulated and a tiny bit broken? For Watts, her family and friends were fundamental in offering perspective.

'Having a good support network was the most important thing for me. Listen to those people. If your friends and family are saying to you, "You are unhappy, get out of there," then do it. It did take me another six months to realise and to reconcile within myself that I needed to go, but they planted the seed.'

Pizer concurs, explaining that there are a few things you can do if you find yourself suffocated by a toxic workplace. Firstly, she says, don't stay there if you don't have to. Listen to the people around you if they say it's not right. Secondly, and perhaps more realistically, there are a few things you can do on the job if leaving is not an option.

'If it's a singular person, find out what triggers [them]. If they're not a morning person, can you organise to meet with them in the afternoon? If they are a numbers person, give them the numbers. Find out what they are after and what they are interested in and work with that. If it's in just one department, you might want to look into taking it up the chain. Focus on the impact on the bottom line and the company's results.'

While Pizer would always encourage an employee to 'minimise the contact with the people who are upsetting [them]', if toxicity is bleeding from the top down, sometimes that is not a feasible option. 'There is safety and power in numbers. If there's a group of you who are disgruntled, complaining together can be much harder to ignore.'

While the nature of most work can be inherently stressful, Pizer says if there's a niggling feeling that something isn't right, then the chances are something needs to change.

'If you know in your heart of hearts that something isn't right, it probably isn't. You're not the problem.'

Here's the thing that has always troubled me: no single experience is all good or all bad. No story is absolute, no tale complete without dashes of nuance and detail and layers. My time in a toxic workplace was terrible, that much I have made clear, but I can't shake the idea that I wouldn't be where I am now without it.

By virtue of having responsibility I didn't think I was qualified for, I became more mature. I met some of my closest friends, who are smart and funny and love reading the same things I do. Hell, I met Michelle, who is almost a firmer fixture in my life than my boyfriend. Sometimes I find myself wondering how much I owe to that time, those contacts, and that job; how much I owe that experience for teaching me everything I never wanted in a workplace.

When we interviewed Gemma Watts about her first job, I asked her the same question. Did she ever feel conflicted about her time in an emotionally abusive workplace for the reason that it's impossible to consider anything as awful in its entirety?

'Was it worth it? I don't know,' Watts said. 'It's hard to say whether things were worth it because you don't know what would have come out of the alternative. I think in my case, it probably was worth it. I really think I did need the six months that followed to figure out what I wanted to do, come up with the game plan, get all of my ducks in a row and go from there. But it's so different for everyone. I'm very grateful I got to do that job and

I learned so much from it. But then, there was some weird shit going on that I should have escaped earlier than I did. It takes a mental toll.'

I wonder, too, if our tendency to glorify experience has a bit – or a lot – to answer for in this context. The minute we decide to enter the workforce, we're told experience is the currency we need; that experience is so valuable that it's the same as being paid well, or enough to reimburse you for your time, energy and mental health. It plays on our biggest insecurity: that experience is the one thing we don't have, and only time spent working will change that. For Petersen, the assumed value of experience works to justify much of the crap work we take on in our twenties.

'This is often the argument that people make to convince themselves that unpaid internships are okay... and unpaid internships are just the furthest end of the spectrum, with all sorts of exploitative work that's sold as "meaningful" or a way to follow your dream. The reality is that these places have realised that people will do this work for very little, and with very little security, and so they offer very little,' she says.

Jamila Rizvi, author of the millennial career manifesto *Not Just Lucky*, says yes, experience is important. However, she agrees with Petersen that the global financial crisis (GFC) of 2008 and the ensuing recession gave birth to an entire generation whose desperation for work was palpable.

'As someone who's worked as a manager and an employer, there is definitely no substitute for experience. That is a fact of workplaces, not just in Australia but everywhere. However, I worry that there are conditions in the labour market at the moment and over the past ten to fifteen years, that mean workplaces are able to take advantage of that fact – and the desperation of young people to get experience – to essentially get free labour,' she says.

'The global financial crisis really hit young people, who went on to study through further education and kept getting educated because it was so hard to make that next jump into paid work. If you look at the unemployment rates of around that time (and the years that followed) it actually hit young people harder than anyone else. There's a generation of young people who graduated from school, university and TAFE in the ten years afterwards who went into workplaces with a level of desperation to prove themselves and get experience. That meant the imbalance of power between the employer and the non-employee, or the hopeful employee, was exacerbated even further.'

The thing we seem to be forgetting about experience in this context is that you can gain and learn from experience without it necessarily needing to be tough or bad. In other words, you can grow from positive, productive, beneficial experience, too. It's like we have conflated negative experience with valuable experience (partly, too, because of the badge of honour associated with rigorous, demanding jobs). We have absorbed this idea that to be young and in the workforce is to have to cop the toxicity because you're a millennial and hey, at least you have a job! It's all part of the package, along with knowing your place, having little power, and having to earn respect to climb the ranks.

In those moments when I wonder if I would still be where I am today without it all, I wonder, too, whether that line of thought has any relevance at all. Perhaps I would be here, perhaps I wouldn't, but perhaps it doesn't matter. Perhaps the most important point is that I should never have been exposed to it at all.

Maybe, in arguing that I wouldn't be here without it, I'm promulgating the narrative that work is the most important thing in a millennial's life and that bad experiences are necessary for career growth. That success should come at any cost. But success *shouldn't* come at any cost. Our careers are not our religions, and our identities are more than what we do for a day job. The more we assume we are our work and our work is us, and the more we encourage a dialogue that says our careers are our currency, the more young people will find themselves trapped in a workplace that is actively doing harm – for who are they, if not for the job title next to their name?

I work, therefore I am. I am, therefore I work.

'I think this is where people get stuck: in jobs that ostensibly fit their "passions", or are "cool" in some way that should be fulfilling, but [that] are toxic – either because of cultures of overwork, under-compensation, or just shitty and inexperienced management,' Petersen argues. 'Oftentimes, we have no reference point for what a healthy working environment might look like, so it's hard to know if it's normal or actually toxic. But yes, we've also been trained to think of our whole lives as leading to "meaningful" work, so it's very difficult to distance ourselves from the job once we achieve it.'

It would be easy to take a simplistic view of work with this in mind: that pursuing passion can get us into trouble. But it's more nuanced than that. Passion isn't a flaw, and finding work you like – *love,* even – can be central to fulfilment. Petersen's point is about being wary of how passion can be abused by the wrong workplace. It is also about being cognisant of how a job does not need to fit your passions and values for it to be right.

Rizvi also believes we struggle to disentangle ourselves from toxic workplaces because of how tightly our identity is tied up with them.

'Millennials as a generation have been raised to have their identity and work more intertwined than other generations. There's a whole host of reasons for that: one of them is that we're having children later, giving us more of a time period where work is an essential focus for us,' she says.

Rizvi says there is one other key reason: the modern-day scapegoat that is technology.

'Technology means working hours bleed into our social hours, which means our work selves bleed into our social selves. You're not leaving work at 5 pm and switching your work self off and your social self on. Rather, you will always be contactable by work, you're always thinking about work. Your personal identity and your work identity become really fused together.'

But just to come full circle, nothing *is* all good or all bad. After all, being invested in your work is certainly not a terrible way to expend your energy.

'There are enormous positives for finding personal value and fulfilment in your work,' Rizvi says. 'I think it's a wonderful thing to pursue work that is not just something that pays you, but something that is worthwhile, something that brings you joy, something that helps you form relationships and something that gives you a sense of self. But that can easily slide into work *becoming* your sense of self. And if work is your sense of self, then anything that threatens that work is really problematic.'

I remember the days when I'd travel home from work feeling sick, or in tears, or so depleted because of built-up anxiety that I would spend the night mute, not knowing what to say or where to start. I remember the days of being told by my family and friends to 'just leave', of being told there's more to life than going to work, of being encouraged to look for new, different and perhaps less 'career' kinds of work until I found myself again.

To leave a job because of unhappiness assumes we all have the privilege of prioritising contentment over money. Few can quit on command, or take extended leave with no preparation. I certainly didn't feel like I could. Despite that, there is merit in having conversations about how much a job is worth, and why we find ourselves so invested in the idea of who we are as workers.

It's a snobbery thing, a late-capitalist thing, yet it's still a thing: as millennials and gen Zers, we tell ourselves our purpose is our career. But what if it didn't have to be?

I thought this was my answer. I thought if our fixation on work lessened, then perhaps we would be less likely to be tied up in workplaces that are toxic. But then a global pandemic hit and, thanks to a spike in unemployment and millions more working from their bedrooms and kitchens, we were working less than ever. Curiously, the focus on who we are as workers did not dissipate, but transformed into conversations about who we are as workers without, well, work to do. Should we all be learning languages? An instrument? How can we be productive and efficient with excess time on our hands? The message public consensus sent us was clear: if we cannot work for income, then we sure as hell better be working on ourselves. The quiet hum of pressure to self-optimise did not exist outside of our conversations about work but deep within them, an extension of the idea that all action we take must be meaningful. That the way we spend our time is central to our worth in the world.

There's something to be said about perspective and identity here. If we were less preoccupied with what our jobs say about us, about how productive we are in and out of work, and a little more focused on what our personalities and fears and hopes say about us, perhaps then our priorities would shift as our identities evolved. If we were less fixated on what our careers say about our social standing, then maybe our workplaces would have no choice but to treat us better, no longer being able to rely on young, desperate, committed employees to do their grunt work for next to nothing. Yes, it took me leaving my job to realise how much I needed to leave. It took space and hindsight, and a clear mind to see that work didn't have to be (and shouldn't be) at the centre of my world if it was beginning to cripple my world. It took me leaving my job to realise that leaving wasn't the end of it all.

My world didn't implode, my identity didn't evaporate and my days kept rolling. I came into my own more without that job than I ever did while I had it.

Leaving wasn't the end of it at all. It happened to be the start of something much greater.

Everything start-ups offer people in their twenties (apart from, you know, proper pay)

- Free yoga!

- Free pizza on every third Friday!

- Personal development sessions in the boardroom at lunchtime! Whatever the fuck they are! Lucky you don't ever take a lunchbreak anyway!

- Weekly all-company newsletters that use the words 'culture' and 'team' and 'KPIs'!

- A 'promotion' without a pay increase!

- A new title for your email signature!

- A new title for your email signature that actually means nothing at all!

- Opportunities to grow and progress through our hierarchical company structure! Just never push us on what that actually means!

- Tampons!

- Pads! Do you prefer pads? We can give you pads!

- Hot-desking! Everybody just loves unpacking and repacking their desk every single day! It's an exercise in creativity! Don't ask why the bosses never do it!

- PYJAMA DAY! Those watermelon-themed jammies can soothe your concerns that we blatantly disregard the pay grade you're supposed to be on!

- Casual-dress Fridays!

- Bring your dog if you like! We'll look after her more than we look after you!

- A day off for your birthday! Just make sure you celebrate your birthday on a day that suits us! (Wednesday, we like Wednesday.)

- Shitty PR packages that turn up to the office that go unclaimed! Here, honey, have some shampoo and four-day-old biscuits!

- A jazzy, employee-of-the-month certificate that comes with no reward at all!

- Friday drinks to distract you from the fact we haven't trained you to do the job we expect you to do from Monday to Friday!

- Friday drinks to distract you from the fact you were always going to be in the office working late anyway!

- Access to your emails over the weekend, too!

- Burnout!

- Fucked sleeping patterns!

- Existential dread!

- Trust issues to last you a lifetime!

- But baby, don't forget about that free yoga!

The space between my fridge and your fridge

I'm one of those people who sucks at little life stuff.

I need to clean the inside of my oven. I need to get my car serviced and fix its broken door. And its air conditioner. And its AUX cord jack. Someday soon, my jumbled mess of jumpers and exercise tights and odd socks – my loose interpretation of what you might call a 'wardrobe' – will swallow me whole and suck me into another dimension. I haven't been to the dentist in . . . well, in a long time, and I'd go to the dentist tomorrow if the fear of telling the dentist how long it's been between visits didn't fill my soul with paralytic fear.

There's the spotty mould growing on the bathroom ceiling that needs to be smacked with bleach. There are the three lightbulbs that blew six months ago, which I could very easily replace with a single supermarket trip but instead, I've spent every night *perishing in darkness.* There's a pair of boots I told myself I'd get re-soled before winter came, but winter came and went (on repeat) and now I have a pair of very lovely, very expensive leather boots that have missed out on four winters in a row because their owner is a lazy sack of potatoes.

Am I lazy? I'm actually not sure if that's the word for it. Am I enveloped by the crumbling decay of my own life? Sure. This shit is ugly and it's annoying and I often find myself muttering 'Where the fuck does all that hair come from?' whenever the sunlight hits the interior floor of my car.

It's fucked. I know. You would seriously think I was bald.

I will never be the woman who goes to the dentist every six months, or who uses a bookmark (in my staunch anti-bookmark defence, folding down pages is efficient and practical and something I give you permission to do with this book). I will never be that person with the label-maker or the perfectly fluffed up couch cushions that you see in Bec Judd's Instagram photos. I could count on one hand the number of times I have made my bed since 2011. One, reader. One measly time. And it was only to catfish my boyfriend into thinking I'm the kind of person who has her shit together enough to make her bed in the morning. It worked, because here he is four years later, finding miscellaneous possessions in our sheets late at night, ruing the day he hit on that blonde girl at a bogan pub on Christmas Eve. Hahahaha. Sucker.

I know other women are similarly afflicted. I see them most weeknights, wandering the aisles of Coles with stunned expressions that indicate, yes, they managed to forget their environmentally friendly green bags for the seventy-second time this year. I see them rocking up to work with a foundation–bronzer cocktail on their neckline because they did their make-up before putting on their tight cream turtleneck top – again. I see them when I look at Zara, who refuses to register her Myki card for automatic top-ups despite regularly promising to do so, resulting in last-minute dashes to the nearest 7-Eleven and us missing our tram every Monday. I see them in my sister Evelyn, who had her car crashed into by a taxi driver and yet never got it repaired because she just *forgot to,* leaving her car with a huge dent in the back and one lucky Melbourne cabbie with a renewed appreciation for procrastinating millennials.

Of course, for every Michelle, Zara and Evelyn – let's call them Micharalyns – there's a woman who's probably spent the entirety of this piece gagging. She's the Bec Judd of little life stuff. She never has regrowth or chipped nails. She has a handwritten diary in her bag at all times. Her tampons and bobby pins are always within arm's reach, no matter where she is or what she's doing. She owns one of those hand-held vacuum thingies AND she actually uses it. When she reaches down the side of her couch, there's not a dust-coated crumb to be found. You could lick the floor under her ottoman, her place is that clean. She gets her *rings cleaned.* And once they're cleaned? She stores them in a *jewellery organiser.*

I have three jewellery organisers. I use zero of them. Instead, locating a matching pair of earrings every morning is an obstacle course designed to derail my day before it's even begun. Is the matching earring on the floor? Is it irretrievably intertwined with a necklace? Is it swimming in a puddle of micellar water? This rescue process consumes about three minutes of my life every morning. That's 1095 minutes, or 18.25 hours, every fucking year. If you think that's enough motivation for me to pause writing this piece, unbox one of my many jewellery caddies and organise my earrings neatly, you'd be wrong. Why? Because I SUCK AT LITTLE LIFE STUFF, DUMMY. PAY ATTENTION.

I digress.

Telling the two kinds of women apart is easy: you just get them to do the fridge test.

Now I say 'test' because it adds a level of formality and legitness to this exercise. But, really, whether you're a Micharalyn or a Bec boils down to how you answer one single question.

THE FRIDGE TEST

Question 1 of 1:
What is in your vegetable crisper right now?

Multiple-choice options:

a. Nothing whatsoever.

b. Something foreign that does not belong there (i.e. bacon, beer, a vague brown liquid of some description).

c. One floppy carrot and half a bag of semi-liquefied spinach leaves.

d. Edible vegetables only.

Results:

a. Apologies, you are a Micharalyn.

b. Apologies, you are a Micharalyn.

c. Oh dear. You are the epitome of a Micharalyn. We might even be best friends. Now let's walk our sad carrots to the nearest compost bin together while Zara pops into 7-Eleven to top up her Myki.

d. You are a Bec. You've always been a Bec. Your children will be Becs. Their children will be Becs, and they'll take pity on my grandchildren when they see their hoverboards have broken down because they missed the advised service dates by twenty-two months.

AMBITION

I regularly promise myself that I'm going to become a Bec. Oh, how I long to be a magical manicured lady like Bec. Every January I proclaim this is the year that I Get My Shit Together, and I become convinced that it's going to happen. By April, the sheen wears off and I realise I haven't entered a single thing into my handwritten diary since an arrogant men's tennis player was scaring ball kids at the Australian Open. By July, I've convinced myself that driving a shitbox around the streets of Melbourne doesn't make me disorganised, it makes me down-to-earth. By October, my tolerance for anything vaguely related to life admin is lower than my tolerance for people who say *The Bachelor* is better than *Love Island* (cut those people straight out of your life – they can offer you nothing of substance and frankly, you'd be better off without their pungent mediocrity).

I have a theory that Becs have more hours in the day than mere muggles like me. That, or they don't waste copious hours every week watching episodes of *Love Island* and promptly scrolling through Twitter to see what other Micharalyns thought of Amy's outburst over Simon's cheating history. (If the latter is true, the fancy nails and perfectly styled cushions probably aren't worth it, anyway. Sorry.)

Marie Kondo's 'Does it spark joy?' movement didn't fix me. My mother's disappointment couldn't fix me. The jabby hunger pangs that strike whenever I open my fridge to find nothing but an abandoned root vegetable haven't fixed me.

And, so, here I am. A Micharalyn, loud and proud, chaotic and grotty. Waving the stain-laden flag of women everywhere who haven't picked up an iron in two weeks. I see you, ladies. Thank Rihanna and all that is godly that we hit our twenties in this era, not the 1950s.

If you're a Bec, I tip my hat to you, m'lady.

Only, not really. Because all of the hats I own have either

disappeared into my wardrobe vortex, or have collapsed and fallen victim to the fast-and-loose storage style I adopt at the faintest whiff of stress.

Let's try again, shall we?

I wave my fridge door at you, Bec. I wave my fridge door at you and let bottles of aioli and soy sauce fly onto the floor. I'd care more about the wastage, but they were definitely out of date anyway.

The things you shouldn't spend your money on in your twenties, and the things you should

Stuff that is totally not worth your sweet, hard-earned doubloons

1. **Instagram followers.** Everyone with a brain can see *precisely* what you've done. Don't bother.

2. **Yet another 'going out' outfit.** For one, if you're anything like us, the outfits you're buying are not going to age well. Secondly, you'll never wear that teeny-tiny bandeau dress again. And third, you're burning the environment to the ground. Try bopping to Drake's latest song with THAT in mind, Sarah.

3. **Six espresso martinis on a night out.** You will somehow manage to drink so many that you will struggle to sleep for a week and swear yourself off espresso martinis for an eternity.

4. **4 am solo Uber rides when you could have gone home at 3 am and split the fare four ways.** $85 on an Uber across the city is not cute. Think, woman! *Think.*

5. **Hungover Uber Eats orders.** Were seven hash browns necessary? And why are you paying $22 for a burger you could make with the ingredients currently in your fridge?

6. **A car that will break down in approximately eighteen months' time.** Look, you're better off saving an extra $2000 and getting a car that won't become the bane of your existence. It sucks, but spending $3500 on a shitty Holden Barina will actually cost you $6000 in the long run. Holden Barinas suck and will ruin your life. Sorry, Holden. (Can you tell Mich is scarred?)

7. **Shitty souvenirs from your Euro gap year.** Nobody will ever use that Venetian masquerade mask, or overpriced leather cardholder, no matter how good they look at the market. Save those twenty euros and spend them on train tickets, because you will absolutely run out of money with three days to go. Your siblings will thank you for not filling their bedrooms with tacky, dust-collecting junk.

8. **Crappy sunglasses.** Buy one good pair! Stop paying for shit ones! Spoiler! They always break!

9. **An F45 membership.** YOU CAN FIND A CHEAPER WAY TO EXERCISE.

10. **Designer perfume.** You can find very pleasantly scented perfumes that cost less than $70. May we recommend Michael Bublé's Rose Gold?

11. **'Skin toners'.** These just dry your face out and make you smell like methylated spirits. Try to tell us we are wrong on this one.

12. **Packet hair dye.** If Zara had the strength, she would show you photos from 2012. She does not have the strength.

AMBITION

13. **$450 on a hairdresser.** This goes both ways, friends. Find the middle ground.

14. **Eyelash extensions.** Seriously, add it up. You're committing yourself to paying $80 every three weeks for the *rest of your life*. They look cute, but do they look *that cute*?

15. **Renting an apartment you can't afford.** 'Affording' your rent means being able to pay it every month and still save money on the side. Are you saving anything right now? If not, downgrade your rental. Your marble benchtop won't put dinner on the table. (Figuratively . . . also, literally.)

16. **A Gucci bag.** Unless you are secretly from the Packer family, you cannot afford a Gucci bag in your twenties. Next.

17. **A $300 bag of cocaine.** See above.

18. **Any form of diet shake, supplement, pill or tea.** Explosive diarrhoea is not pretty or cute, no matter how attractive those captions and selfies make it look.

19. **Expensive bottles of wine.** Aldi wine is the fucking best and costs like $5 a bottle. Fight us.

Stuff that will make your life a million
times better, because we are all about
INVESTMENT

1. **A silk pillowcase.** The hype is true. It will make your hair très shiny. Worth it.

2. **A pet.** As if you need us to even explain this one to you. (Actually, we may still need to explain it to Zara. Zara, I have three words for you: 'furry unconditional love'.)

The Space Betw

een

3. **Travel.** Yes, saving is good, but this is one of the only times in your life where you will (probably) have zero dependants. GO EXPLORE. Fly across the world, sail around coastlines, bus between cities. Fall in love with a backpacker! Go three days without showering! You will never regret travelling.

4. **Psychologist sessions.** Your mind is bloody important. Look after it.

5. **An anxiety blanket.** Even if you don't have anxiety . . . you should get an anxiety blanket. We recommend lying underneath an anxiety blanket while eating a bowl of carbonara.

6. **A great pair of jeans.** Don't skimp on jeans! If you find a pair you love, and they cost a week's rent, we say fuck it. You're going to wear them every second day for the next decade, so go right ahead.

7. **Cute lingerie.** Fact: you are never too broke for a set of lacy undies and a bra that make you feel as confident and regal as Lizzo.

8. **Sunscreen.** USE FUCKING SUNSCREEN. EVERY DAY. A GOOD BRAND, TOO. THAT IS ALL.

9. **Moisturiser.** Okay so that wasn't all. While we're talking about sunscreen, why not actually hydrate that damn face of yours?

10. **A high-end lipstick.** You just need one shade but make it a banger. The fancy ones are awfully creamy and – dare we say it – worth it.

11. **Manicures and pedicures.** Okay, so we aren't talking about those ridiculous $100 manis, but a decent $50 mani? Abso-fucking-lutely! It's a great way to have a little me-time. You're worth it, etc.

12. **A gym membership.** Okay, so let's be real: $20 a fortnight is a little more appropriate than what you're spending on F45. Plus, you spend that amount on almond milk lattes every work week and we both know it. Going to the gym is brilliant for your body and mind. Tick, tick.

13. **Good wireless headphones.** They block out the rest of the world when you need it most, and make a gym session go at least 187 per cent quicker. Best enjoyed with a Taylor Swift playlist. Don't you dare judge us.

14. **A good vacuum cleaner.** Boring? Yes. Essential from the day you move out? Absolutely. You do NOT want to live in a dusty apartment, and you will never ever regret spending money on a high-powered vacuum cleaner. The more expensive you go, the more you will enjoy cleaning. It's science. Look it up.

15. **A steamer.** The fairy godmother of all appliances. That is all.

16. **Ambulance insurance.** Don't be the person who dislocates their jaw by yawning too widely and then has to spend $1300 on getting to the hospital. Nobody wants to be that person. (Mich was that person.)

17. **Car insurance.** Sensing a theme here?

18. **The dentist.** Because teeth.

19. **Books.** The written word needs your support. Writers need your support! This is totally unbiased! Not a thinly veiled plea at all! But seriously: books will enrich your life and broaden your perspective on the world. Money is never wasted on books. Never, ever, ever.

A rough and tumble on . . .
rejection

On Sat, 4 Jul 2020 at 12:32 PM,
Zara McDonald <zaramcdonald@shameless.com> wrote:

>>> Look, I don't know where we should start with this, but I'll try here:
    If I were to ask you what career rejection hurt the most, what would
    you say? (I ask, but it's a leading question because I already have a hunch
    about what you'll say.)

On Sat, 4 Jul 2020 at 12:51 PM,
Michelle Andrews <michelleandrews@shameless.com> wrote:

>>> What a FUN QUESTION!
    Ah rejection. I still remember the sting of being the only girl in my year
    not to be invited to Jess S.'s eighth birthday party. Also, being turned
    down by a boy at Mount Waverley train station because he 'didn't realise
    I had buck teeth' from my MySpace photo.
    But the *career rejection* that hurt the mooooost?
    The one at Mamamia. Lol. You?

On Sat, 4 Jul 2020 at 1:16 PM,
Zara McDonald <zaramcdonald@shameless.com> wrote:

>>> Yeah, same. Obviously.

At the risk of being accused of burying the lead and being annoying, let me jump straight into recounting what actually happened before we go anywhere else.

So we had the idea for *Shameless* in mid to late 2017, I think? We had dipped our toes into the crazy world of podcasting here and there (we did a fifteen-minute *Bachelor* recap pod once that still lives on the internet, which is a fact that makes us both want to die. It was bad. Very bad). While we really enjoyed it, we felt a celebrity and pop culture podcast that spoke about more than just drunken rose ceremonies was bound to be even better. We knew we were green to the broadcasting and podcast space, but what we lacked in experience we made up for in enthusiasm, so we pitched it anyway. We met with sales experts within the company to make sure it would be commercially viable, we sat down together to record a thirty-minute pilot episode, we even brainstormed ideas for segments and jingles. We were committed. We were all in. Okay, you take it from here.

On Sat, 4 Jul 2020 at 1:25 PM,
Michelle Andrews <michelleandrews@shameless.com> wrote:

>>> I knew you'd make me do the dirty work.

I remember when we were brainstorming names for the podcast I put forward *The Blue Tick* – as in, the little blue symbol indicating someone is verified on Insta or Twitter – which, on reflection, sounds like a nasty STI you'd get from a dude you met in a London hostel. I'm pretty bloody glad you steered me far, far away from that name (and other total duds like *The Fame Game*) and onto *Shameless* instead. Looking back, I don't even think *Shameless* was our idea – it was our friend Rachel Wagner's. Kudos, Rach.

ANYWAY. Our pitch was accepted and we were told to prepare for a January launch date to coincide with the US awards-show season. All of our co-workers were told in an editorial meeting that we'd be hosting a shiny new celebrity podcast in 2018 and we received one-on-one training with the Head of Podcasts. I was positively BUBBLING with excitement to have our own proper podcast and be Proper Media People.

That is, until we got that email . . .

(Dun dun dunnnnnnnn. Do you like how I'm building suspense, here? No? It's irritating? TOO BAD THESE ARE MY EMAILS.)

On Sat, 4 Jul 2020 at 1:42 PM,
Zara McDonald <zaramcdonald@shameless.com> wrote:

>>> Ah yes, that email. I remember *that* email well. It's funny, the small things you retain from a big moment. I remember exactly where I was: I was travelling across the Bolte Bridge in Melbourne one evening after work. My best friend Sammy was driving, and our friend Jordan was in the back. Anyway, I looked down at my phone and saw I had like seven missed calls from you. I called you back, and you were kind of breathless on the phone. (I love when two people tell the same story because I wonder if you'll go on to dispute that.)

That email had landed in our inbox.

The podcast, just weeks from launch, had been pulled. No detailed explanation was given (resources, maybe?), but one stood out to us more than anything: the idea was good. You guys as hosts, though? Eh, it may not work.

I have to be honest, I was pretty shattered. The thing about my relationship with rejection is that I don't dwell on it, and that's not some crazy, misguided humblebrag. It's a self-defence mechanism. I don't dwell on rejection because I know if I let it, it could eat me alive. I think my ego is so fragile that sometimes if I let certain things in, I would never shake them. It sounds dramatic (maybe/probably/definitely it is), but it's all a processing thing.

The funny part about this rejection was that I *did* dwell on it. I dwelt on it spectacularly. I didn't understand why exactly it had been pulled. I felt like we'd been strung along and I felt like we'd put our whole selves into a project that was tossed away without a second thought.

With hindsight, it's interesting to me that we resented the eleventh-hour pull because of all the work we had put in, but we didn't resent (as much, at least) the inference that we might not be good at this job. We didn't resent it because we believed the higher-ups when they inferred we may not be ready. I think they hit us at our biggest insecurity: *Why the fuck would anyone listen to us?*

On Sat, 4 Jul 2020 at 2:01 PM,
Michelle Andrews <michelleandrews@shameless.com> wrote:

>>> Oh, absolutely. It knocked me around for sure. I remember I was sitting on my dad's couch and looking out onto the summer skyline with this sense of perplexity. I had been so, *so* excited to try something new. Knowing that they liked our idea but not necessarily *us* was what worried me the most; I was convinced that they would take our pitch and give it to two other willing employees.

I think I felt embarrassment, too. I have the world's biggest mouth, so had told everyone from my sisters to my schoolfriends to my pet dog Peanut about our upcoming podcast, and having to inform them all that it wasn't going ahead because, in part, *we weren't adequate hosts* was slightly yuck. I suffer from imposter syndrome at the best of times and this experience sent my paranoia that I'm just not good enough into overdrive. I couldn't stop thinking, *Well, the people making these decisions are older and have far more experience in the industry than us – if they don't think we're good enough, they're probably right.*

I kept replaying in my head all the times I'd stumbled over my words or didn't perform well in recordings, as if making mistakes in the past was confirmation that I'd never be 'up to it' in the future. I kept looking to other hosts within the network – our co-workers and friends – and wondering what the people in charge saw in them that they didn't see in us. Was there a quality that you and I lacked so deeply that it simply couldn't be trained or taught?

But even then, I couldn't shake one core belief: there is literally only one way to get better and that's to keep practising. We weren't going to become great broadcasters by sitting behind laptops all day; we needed to hop behind microphones. And if the idea was good and we were given time to improve, who knew what could come of it? I couldn't bear the thought of our idea being given to other hosts. I think there was a fire within me that wanted to prove people wrong – not in a 'you're stupid' way, but in a 'you really underestimated us' way.

That was the driving force behind us replying to Mamamia's rejection email with a request to pursue the podcast on our own, outside of work hours. We had no bloody idea how to record, edit or produce audio, of course, but that was a speed bump we were willing to navigate later with the not-always-very-helpful aid of YouTube tutorials.

I wanted, desperately, to show the people who told us 'no' that they had made a mistake. Maybe that's immature, or maybe it's just human, but I had a healthy thirst for revenge. Even now, with all this time and space since, I want to prove those people wrong. It's like my fuel.
I know you craved similar things – do you still?

**On Sat, 4 Jul 2020 at 2:14 PM,
Zara McDonald <zaramcdonald@shameless.com> wrote:**

>>> A little bit, yeah. I'd be lying if I said us doggedly pursuing the podcast alone wasn't part revenge, part fear. Like you, I was scared that if we didn't fill this gap in the market, someone else would, and I was a tiny bit desperate to prove that we were capable of *something*.

Rejection does funny things to you. Because, for all of our relentless work on the podcast, we weren't necessarily confident about it. We weren't even sure it would work. All we knew was we had nothing to lose and every-thing to gain. Without sounding preachy – or truthfully, like I have any idea what I am talking about – I think there is benefit in looking at rejection from that perspective. (PS: This doesn't extend to that kid who rejected you at the train station because of your teeth. More than definitely leave that one alone.)

It's funny though, Mich, because the difficulties didn't necessarily stop after that. There was the time we forgot to push 'record' on an episode, another episode we sent live with a glaring editing error we couldn't fix for twenty-four hours because we didn't know how, countless wasted hours spent setting up podcasting equipment because we had no idea which cord went where and other days – multiple, in fact – when we recorded an entire segment only to realise it was too weak and we'd have to re-record. I remember, too, charging sponsors ridiculously low rates for ad spots, and wondering how we were ever going to make *Shameless* An Actual Thing that we could leave our jobs for. None of this touches on the many, many weeks our downloads would drop or plateau and we would rack our brains about how to grow them again.

With all this in mind, we wanted, so badly, for the podcast to be picked up by a network so we could have help (!!!) on the production side, but no one wanted it. Did that make you doubt what we had? That nobody else seemed to consider it worthy or legitimate?

On Sat, 4 Jul 2020 at 2:36 PM,
Michelle Andrews <michelleandrews@shameless.com> wrote:

>>> Is it arrogant if I say no? Once we got going, I kind of stopped caring about what the 'industry professionals' working for big networks thought of us. I just figured we knew how to speak to people our age better than a fifty-year-old ever could. We were creating content for people like us, and pretty quickly I realised that's the magic ingredient. It's something that can't be replicated by a bunch of people in a boardroom, no matter

how intently they scroll through @TheFatJewish's Instagram feed or study what entertainment stories are trending on Twitter that day. The greenness of not even knowing that microphone stands are extendable (yes, really) was actually on our side in every possible way. There were dozens of Aussie podcasts that screamed out to women over thirty, but for those of us who were trudging through university or squirming in their first graduate job? There was zilch. Nada. I respect experience, of course, but at this point in time – where new media was eclipsing the old – that was the difference. It turned out we weren't the only ones with no goddamn idea what we were doing: everyone else was utterly clueless, too.

I will always be surprised that Mamamia didn't want the podcast, even after it launched and had carved out its own little space in the podcasting world. I think that, when we went into meetings with HR to discuss our places at the company in those final days, I always expected them to turn around and offer to bring *Shameless* under the Mamamia Podcast Network banner. I know that we both desperately wanted that, and would have replied with a big fat yes before they'd even finished asking the question. And yet, that was never the case. If anything, it was kind of the opposite, and the podcast was merely a few months old when we decided the only real option was to walk away from our jobs.

What we didn't realise then was that each rejection was actually a radiant blessing. You and I are lucky that we got 'no' after 'no', because every single one led us to where we are today.

If we had pulled *Shameless* under our employer, our roles as podcast hosts would have been collapsed into our existing roles, and we likely wouldn't have seen a cent of the profits. Signing with one of the many networks we reached out to wouldn't have been much better, either; it would have meant giving away fifty per cent of our commercial revenue – something that makes me royally pissed off as a creator who knows how much work goes into getting an episode into the feeds every week. Being told no or, as was most often the case, having our emails completely ignored, was a sign from a Podcasting God (probably, like, the anonymous dude who hosts *Casefile* or something) that doing this independently was the only way forward. I wish I could tell the Michelle of 2018 to back herself. To keep doing what she was doing because it was going to work: hanging those amateurish posters up on the back of university bathroom stalls, posting Kim Kardashian memes into an Instagram void, looking for tiny windows of opportunity to push the podcast through, every single day. I wish I could tell her that everything would pan out just fine. Actually, much, much better than fine. It would pan out like this: she's co-authoring a book. Co-directing a media company. Co-parenting a podcast that is kind of like her first baby.

Two years later, I look at what you and I have done together, Zara, and I feel proud. I'm glad we didn't let the many 'no's defeat us. I think having you by my side gave me the courage and strength to keep going, even when I felt like a child playing make-believe. Without you, I'd probably be stuck in a vicious cycle of self-doubt and worry, consumed by the omnipresent question marks from the people around me.

Because here's the thing: *nobody really knows* what ideas will work and what won't. Sure, we can have our hunches. We can have our instincts. But none of us *know*. Even the world's most successful entrepreneurs have failed and faltered. Their ideas have bombed and sunk. But that's what makes them successful – they've got lots of ideas, and they're willing to give each decent one a go regardless of the outcome. Those successful people have, in their time, probably also rejected ideas that have gone on to be brilliant – ideas that passed them by because they didn't sense the pulse of the moment.

I have no doubt that you and I will reject some great ideas simply because we are busy pressing our index fingers to other things, wondering if the pulse is somewhere up here, or down there. Someone might come to us and present her shiny jewel of insight and creativity, and we will shrug when we should be jumping at the chance to help her make it into a ring. If that does happen one day, I'd want the young woman holding the precious gem to just make the goddamn thing herself. I'd want her to pull out her toolkit and get to work, because if she sees something in it, the chances are someone else will too. We're all feeling for hard stones in the ground, trying to figure out what's a rock and what's a diamond. Do you love your idea? Well, say yes to yourself and polish that stone until it shines. Say 'yes' to yourself again and again, especially when everyone else is telling you 'no'.

If you could go back to the Zara and Michelle of January 2018 and tell them anything, what would you say?

On Sat, 4 Jul 2020 at 2:47 PM,
Zara McDonald <zaramcdonald@shameless.com> wrote:

>>>   That's an interesting question. What would I actually say to the twenty-three-year-old versions of us if I were given the chance? Truthfully, my first thoughts are buried in clichés and I'm betting you know exactly the ones. 'When one door closes . . .' or 'Everything happens for a reason' or 'This will be the making of you.'

The (annoying but) bottom line is they are all absolutely true. Those numerous rejections *did* happen for a reason, a million doors *did* open when one slammed in our face and I think building this alone *did* make us into stronger, better, more thoughtful people. Beyond that, though, I'd tell us to harness naivety and blind belief. That successful people don't have a blueprint or much of a path, or even a better idea than the next person. I would tell us what Business Chicks founder Emma Isaacs once told us when we interviewed her: that the only thing that's common to the people who find success is their unwavering ability to back themselves.

Of course, you're totally right: it's a little easier to back yourself when there's two of you backing each other. The fact that I had you and you had me meant whenever we did start to waver, or whenever self-doubt or confusion crept into our thoughts and conversations, we had someone to catch us. We had our arms at the ready to catch each other.

Above all, I would sit us down and tell us that just because big media players saw no value in what we wanted to create and just because established brands couldn't jump on board with our vision and enthusiasm, doesn't mean the ideas were any less worthy.

After all, that's the reason the idea could work in the first place: their blind spots are creating the holes you are just about to fill.

So hurry up and fill the damn things.

The space between success and sacrifice

— ZARA —

It was lunchtime on a grey Monday in July of 2019 and Michelle and I had just completed two interviews for what was then *Shameless*'s 'In Conversation' arm of the podcast. Earlier that morning we had sat down with Business Chicks founder Emma Isaacs, before heading into the Melbourne CBD to interview Cyan Ta'eed, founder of Envato, Hey Tiger and Milkshake.

The two of us jumped into a lift, lugging our recording equipment behind us in a suitcase that was not built for the load we expected it to carry. We waited for the doors on the lift to close, and then we looked at each other. I opened my mouth to speak.

'I hear stuff like that and immediately think I don't have it in me. Do you?'

As is customary with most of our conversations, I didn't need to give Mich much context for her to understand the point I was getting at.

'I absolutely don't think I do either.'

We were about four months into running our own business, having launched the podcast some fourteen months before.

While there was always an implicit (and contractual, thanks very much) understanding that *Shameless* was our long game, we had never deeply discussed what our work lives would look like in five, ten or fifteen years' time. The two of us had never sat down and discussed how much of ourselves we would be willing to give over to our jobs, or how much of our lives we were prepared to sacrifice for success. The conversation we had in twenty-five words or fewer in that lift was around sacrifice and balance. It was a tiny acknowledgement of something much greater. *How much will you give yourself over to this?*

We had spent our morning asking these wildly successful, wildly kind women about what changes in your life when work becomes your beginning, middle and end game. Neither Ta'eed nor Isaacs were delicate in communicating their reality: their lives looked different now to how they had before they became entrepreneurs. They loved the lives they had built, they told us, but they quickly learned that the more they leaned into their work, the fewer priorities they had time for.

'I'm yet to meet a really successful human who's been able to have everything,' Isaacs told us that morning, when we pushed her on those concepts of balance, time and knowing whom to give your energy to and when. 'Something has to give. I have spent the last twenty years studying successful people, meeting them and hanging out with them and no one has been able to do that. I don't have much of a social life. I made the decision that what's important to me in my life is spending enough time with my children so that they never feel like Mum had this great career but she was never around. That means oftentimes I don't go out at all. I have a few very close friends who I love dearly but don't see as much as I'd like to. I made a decision that that was what was important to me, because you just can't have everything.'

Hours later, Ta'eed echoed much of what Isaacs said, almost unprompted.

'It is incredibly tiring. It is not easy,' she said, of spending much of her time working. 'It is not elegant. There's this idea that somehow it's this effortless life and it is very, very difficult. There is a reason why there's that "man in the arena" quote. One of the reasons that quote resonates with me is because it's bloody hard. You have incredible highs and lows. And I get very, very, very tired. That's okay, that's what I've chosen to do. I get a chance to test myself, but it's hard. It's not easy.'

With some digging, I later found the quote Cyan was referring to. It was from Theodore Roosevelt:

> It is not the critic who counts; not the man who points out how the strong man stumbles, or where the doer of deeds could have done them better. The credit belongs to the man who is actually in the arena, whose face is marred by dust and sweat and blood . . .

Her point was a worthy one. Who wouldn't prefer to be the one down and dirty in the arena, doing the grunt work? Is life not about being the fighter and the worker? About testing ourselves, about sacrifice, about seeing what we are capable of when everything feels like a challenge?

It's just that, as the lift doors closed on Mich and me, the one thought I couldn't help coming back to was this: the life both Isaacs and Ta'eed describe appears electrifying and fulfilling and full of triumph and accomplishment.

But what if I didn't want any of it?

Maybe it was the timing of it all, too. When we were recording those episodes, I was struggling. The way I described it to a friend was that I felt like I was sitting on a see-saw. Instead of the see-saw being for two people, though, I told her to imagine me on one end and twenty different things on separate planks at the other, all overlapping, crisscrossing, lifting and falling. I was so time-poor navigating my relatively new working arrangements, and it felt as though whenever I directed my weight somewhere, it was at the expense of something else. The minute I channelled my time and energy into one relationship in my life, another was ignored or forgotten. I didn't know where to invest my weight, because it felt like I was failing whichever way I turned.

On reflection, there were definite doses of drama and self-flagellation about the whole exchange, but it wasn't a temporary situation I was trying to describe: I had been grappling with the guilt of feeling absent from my own life for many months before the lift crisis of that Monday in July. What I didn't tell her about were the times my chest would constrict, or the days I felt a tiny bit breathless, or the moments I felt the weight of stress blanket me to the point of mental paralysis.

My reality wasn't an unusual one. I simply didn't know how to give myself over to my work and keep everything else afloat. I could not shake the feeling that the more time I gave to my job, someone and something was inevitably being left behind. Truthfully, I still can't.

A couple of years ago, I remember Mich came to work with an analogy from her psychologist that she found helpful.

> You're given twelve oranges and four baskets. Based on how much mental energy you give something, how do you divide your oranges between the 'Work', 'Family', 'Friends'

and 'Me' baskets? Are they evenly spread? Do some win out over the others? Who is the biggest loser of all?

In the years since, I've used this analogy as a method of self-check-in. How does my own life look from this vantage point? Where is my energy being poured, and how do my oranges fall? Where are my blind spots?

If I were to sit down with you now and lay out my baskets and oranges, I would say seven-and-a-half oranges are in work, two are in friends, two are in family and the remaining half an orange is for myself. I wish they were more evenly distributed, or that there was a way for every basket to be filled with my energy, time and presence in a way that represents how equally important they are all to me.

The reality is, at twenty-six, almost all my time cascades into work. It is my North Star, very often the thing I dream about and invariably the reason I wake. I am happy and fulfilled but I feel *guilty*. The internal and lingering conflict eating at me is this: What if I'm actually doing it all wrong? What if this isn't, at all, what your twenties are for?

Everyone tells you your twenties will be plagued with self-doubt and self-consciousness. They also warn you that no one *actually* knows what they are doing. That yes, people will pretend, will try to fool you with their bravado and their ego, but don't be a sucker for the charade. I just never took that to mean that I would be racked with guilt and worry every time I made a decision. I never expected to be such a casualty of comparison.

Am I spending too much time with my boyfriend? Are all my friends getting the perfect amounts of love, care and attention?

Should I be funnelling more time and energy into work, or less? Do I see my family enough? Do they know I care? Am I going out too much? Not enough? Just enough? What does that even mean?

It doesn't help that a core part of my job involves spending time on my phone (too much, if you ask the devil-like Screen Time settings on my iPhone) watching the shiniest parts of other people's lives unfold in real time. I watch their perceived priorities play out across their Instagram stories, noting down where they spend their work lunches and their weeknights, their weekends or their holidays. I spend my time wondering how they find the time to see all their friends, save all their money and invest in their work. While we lament social media's propensity to make us feel lesser, we don't often mention how it can warp our perspective on how to *live*.

One of the major threads that surfaced in our conversations with Isaacs and Ta'eed was about the necessity of sacrifice when it comes to finding some elusive fragment of success. But that's the thing about living performatively on social media: we don't see sacrifice. None of us are capturing the Saturday nights at home, or the weeknights we don't see our friends because we're working late again, or the moments we feel pulled in so many directions it renders us immobile.

When I found myself halfway through writing this essay, I kept coming back to the same core question. Our lives, as twenty-somethings of this generation, certainly aren't harder than those of any other generation before us. But what makes that sense of being overwhelmed feel so different for us? What makes us so hyperaware of our own vexed priorities? Why do we seem to be drowning in the push and pull of our passions and responsibilities? I ended up calling my mum mid-sentence. Did she, at my age, feel similar to me? Does she remember feeling conflicted about where she channelled her energy, and who she gave her time to?

Yes, she said. Of course she did. But the nature of her priorities was different. (She was speaking generally, of course. My mother is no voice of her generation, as much as she would likely pay me to put that in print.) Work mattered to her, but not to the extent it matters to me.

'You have to understand, Zara, we were some of the first ones to be told we could have a career. We wanted to jump off that cliff, but we wanted to do it gently, and slowly.'

In short, they hadn't seen many others jump. So, she said, she waddled down the cliff face as cautiously as she could. She felt the pull between her friends and her family, but not so much for her career – it was nurtured, for sure, but it was not the biggest part of her identity.

'Maybe we expect more of ourselves now,' she reflected, 'because there are just more things to be invested in.'

More opportunities to find fulfilment, more ways to spend our time and our energy. More ways to do it right, but also more ways to feel like we are doing it wrong.

In the year or so since Mich and I stumbled into that lift and broached, for the first time, how we wanted our work lives to look, we've both spent time reflecting on why we found ourselves so affronted by the concept of pure, unadulterated sacrifice. In that moment, we were shrouded in guilt because sacrifice had already infiltrated our lives. Is this what our twenties are for? Should we be striving for a greater sense of balance than we're currently finding? *Your twenties*, folklore says, *those are the years where you have all the fun.* The external pressure for our twenties to be carefree and playful is suffocating, and not our reality at all. Inevitably, we found ourselves fretting over this one idea: if the need to sacrifice, or the struggle to manage priorities, did not dissipate over time, then would the guilt ever subside?

I wish I could say that in writing this down and having a year to mull over it all, I have come to some kind of firm conclusion about time and priorities and guilt. I wish I could tell you what it's like to feel as though you're spiralling, and counsel you on how to pull yourself out of the vortex. But maybe therein lies the point: maybe there is no resolution or conclusion because our priorities are fluid, our energy in flux and our time, while constant, subject to both of those things. What keeps me warm when I feel waves of that rapacious guilt is the knowledge that nothing good can be done by halves and that, realistically, throwing yourself into something is always, always, *always* going to come at the expense of something else. Sacrifice, too, I've since learned – in no matter the shape or form it takes in our lives – is crucial to progressing anything: career, friendships, relationships.

In the past year I have come to understand the necessity of sacrifice and the surety of the accompanying guilt, but one thing I could not stop thinking about was whether the guilt lessened with age and time and experience. I decided to check back in with both Isaacs and Ta'eed, almost a year after we first chatted. I sent them both an email and asked: If the natural need to make sacrifices doesn't ever dissipate, does the guilt?

Both had marginally different advice to leave me stewing on. Isaacs wanted me to stop focusing on the guilt around sacrifice, and instead focus on the privilege of sacrifice. As in, *Hey, at least you're passionate about something!*

'A huge part of me wants to say, "Gah! Stop even thinking about this! What a huge privilege it is for us to have found something we're so passionate about so early in our lives",' she wrote to me. 'Most spend their entire lifetimes searching to have the same professional satisfaction and fulfilment, falling short and forever seeing work as just work. Can we reframe this construct of "I work therefore I sacrifice" into "Aren't I lucky to be creating? Creating a space to thrive, creating something I'm proud of, creating a legacy, creating financial freedom so I can truly live the life I want..." Working so hard throughout my twenties set me up for the myriad opportunities I now enjoy in my forties and I would not change that for a thing.'

Meanwhile, Ta'eed says getting older comes with a better and more inherent understanding of who you are and what you want. And once that happens? Well, there goes the guilt and the need to feel present in all aspects of our lives.

'I worked hard throughout my twenties – well let's be honest, I've worked hard pretty much constantly since my early twenties. I feel like when we tell women they need balance in all areas that sets us all up for guilt and failure,' she wrote. 'I have two priorities: my family and my work. That is okay with me, because I really love both those things and I'm not willing to be "just okay" at either. The people I'm close to know I work hard so I can't always see them, but the intensity of my love and loyalty are more important to them. You can't give yourself fully to too many things. You can probably only be great at a couple! Once you figure out what you want your life to be about, you understand yourself better and the decisions get a lot easier.'

I guess there are two lines of thought that leaves me with: understand that balance will never come, but you'll get better at nutting out your priorities, and feel grateful that you have enough to pour yourself into that you have the power to make priorities in the first place. My baskets will have *something* in them always, and that in itself is notable.

The more I stewed on these conclusions, the more I considered that perhaps, in all my fixation on sacrifice, priorities and guilt,

I had ignored something that Ta'eed and Isaacs had tried to tell me from the start. Both worked through their twenties, and neither seemed to regret any of it.

I wasn't affronted by sacrifice because I wasn't sure it was what I wanted, I was affronted by sacrifice because I wasn't sure if work was the thing I was meant to spend my twenties chasing. But who is to say your twenties aren't for doggedly pursuing your career? Who is to say your twenties aren't for blindly wandering the world? Who is to say your twenties aren't for falling in love and building a home? Who is to say any of it is right, or any of it is wrong?

If twenty-six-year-old me were back in that lift, I would shake my own shoulders. I would tell myself to do what I enjoy and follow what fulfils me: to be selfish and to use the glorious space of my twenties to chase the stuff I love.

Today, that stuff is my work. And tomorrow? Tomorrow, who knows what my heart will chase when the sun comes up.

The space between the next rung on the ladder and the view from here

— MICHELLE —

I have long obsessed over the shape of my career.

I'm passionate. Ambitious. Competitive. When you're a woman, it can be a little dangerous to ascribe those labels to yourself (*Women are supposed to be polite and mild! Like a milky cup of English breakfast tea!*) but for me it's the truth.

As a child I lusted after a life as an actress, and regularly thrust my amateur movie scripts in the faces of my parents and siblings. When I was a teenager, I longed to be a professional netballer, filling car rides to school with feverish analysis of the statistics from last night's game. By the time I had discovered alcohol and boys, I craved the glamour of being a magazine editor with click-clacky heels and a shiny handbag. Despite magazines dying faster than my proclivity for Thursday nights fuelled by Passion Pop Sunrises (Not A Thing in 2013 and certainly Not A Thing now), I punched out sassy blog posts about Mimco clutches and shaggy-haired fuck-boys, figuring that if my university degree wouldn't land me a job, perhaps my thoughts on overpriced accessories and dating would.

AMBITION

I approach my passions with a perfectionistic tenacity that can drain the people around me. With the exception of general life admin, I am diligent about being *good at work*. This all means I'm a greedy boss's dream. It's why I managed to secure promotions relatively young, because I was hell-bent on climbing up the career ladder at the expense of my sanity.

It would be wonderful to work four hours overtime, for no extra pay! Absolutely!

I'd be more than happy to complete this task, which was assigned to you and is not in my job description, and later pretend it was you who did it all along! Of course I'll do that, because I have a pitiful need for you to notice me!

I can think of nothing more delightful than sacrificing my Christmas morning, my birthday dinner and any semblance of a personal life so I can help you make millions of dollars while I languish on $40,000 a year! IT IS MY HONOUR, YOUR MAJESTY. HERE! HAVE ALL OF MY LUNCHBREAKS TOO! I DON'T NEED THEM! I AM NOT WORTHY! I WILL STARVE FOR YOU!

By the age of twenty-two I was the weekend editor of Mamamia which was, at the time, the country's most popular women's website. I was sitting in on the big meetings with the department heads, chipping in my (retrospectively) ignorant and irrelevant ideas on what the average Australian mother of two would like to read about on her Tuesday wee-break from the kids. On occasion, I was trusted with the content direction of the website for entire weekends.

It was 2016, and in 2016 I might have shrugged and told you I had simply found something I was good at. On reflection, my success at Mamamia boiled down to two things:

1. At twenty-two, I had the energy and freedom to care so much about meaningless work stuff, like how many people

read my opinion piece on that bogan *Married at First Sight* contestant. I had the time to analyse our most-read stories and pick up trends about what topics and headlines sang to our readers. I didn't have to go home and whip up spag bol for four, so I could easily sit at my laptop and learn the formula for readership success. It wasn't tricky when you took the time to learn the patterns. It just took an extra dollop of investment – something the vast majority of people in that workplace, with more pressing priorities and responsibilities, couldn't give.

2. I was handed Zara's magnificent brain on a platter as the senior weekend writer and was able to pick it for ideas and pitches whenever I pleased. We naturally fell into a routine: I found the angles and headlines that would get people on the website, while Zara made sure we didn't wander head-first into a defamation case with that *Married at First Sight* contestant.

That was the beauty of being in my early twenties and editing a women's website that demanded my time like an energy-sapping toddler: I was always available, I was always on call. If click-driving news about a *Bachelor* break-up broke when nobody was manning the website, I was the first to pull out my laptop and type with the urgency of someone writing about literally anything other than a *Bachelor* break-up. If I scrolled past a typo on the Instagram feed or a bin fire in the Facebook comments, I jumped at the chance to fix it. I saw my KPIs and daily readership targets like the ultimate challenge: I was hell-bent on achieving them wherever and whenever I could.

My phone was always on, its battery drained by endless email notifications and Slack pings. I didn't take many holidays because, in my mind, taking a break from work was synonymous with not caring about my job enough. When I left the company in 2018, they had to pay me out for more than a month's worth of untaken leave.

In those embryonic stages of my career, I worked through three months of acute glandular fever (after looking at my blood test results, one GP told me my mono constituted a 'ten out of ten' for gross saliva-borne diseases). With the exception of one week of forced leave – when I finally decided to put my big-girl pants on and book an appointment with a psychologist – I worked through some pretty dark days with anxiety. I even worked through hideous bouts of asthma, including one particularly concerning shift in 2017 when, despite experiencing a severe respiratory attack that was non-responsive to my medication, I worked my full eight hours before taking an Uber to the nearest hospital. Upon stumbling into the emergency room, I collapsed.

With the gift of time and a little more maturity, that all seems ridiculous. I'm stunned that I would so flagrantly risk my own health in a quest for my bosses' adoration, but being a twenty-two-year-old editor at a women's media company was my identity.

I'm not alone in this. I know so many people in their twenties who see their work as a mirror to their value; the job title in their email signature is more important than what clothing labels they wear, or what car they drive. The *Shameless* community is brimming with enterprising young women. My siblings and friends are very much stuck in a cycle of worrying about where they'll be in twelve months, in two years, in ten. The notion that millennials and gen Zers are inherently lazy is, to be blunt, bullshit.

When I turned twenty-three, my most pressing worry was, 'What will I achieve this year?' I was so intent on climbing up and up and up, racing to achieve something new and shiny before the next birthday arrived and my achievements were diluted with time.

The fear of stumbling tugged at my ponytail whenever I saw a '30 under 30' list. It was there whenever I spotted the labels 'bestselling author' and 'entrepreneur' side by side in someone's Instagram bio. It was there whenever I heard that the new prime-time hosts on a popular radio station were barely a day over twenty.

Each birthday brought with it a renewed pressure. Had I achieved enough in the last twelve months? Was I where I should be at twenty-three? Twenty-four? Twenty-five?

Life felt like a never-ending season of *The Amazing Race*. I could hear the clock ticking and my ragged panting, only I had no idea what I was actually chasing.

One of my dear friends, Laura Henshaw, is one of the most conventionally successful people I know. By her mid-twenties, she had built a wildly popular online fitness community and food brand, Keep It Cleaner, and co-authored a bestselling young-adult book. With more than a quarter of a million followers on Instagram, she's one of the most influential voices of our generation in Australia. Did I mention she's also on the cusp of completing her law degree? Oh, and she's a model. If she weren't so bloody delightful, generous and intelligent, it would be rather tempting to hate her.

When we first invited Laura onto an 'In Conversation' episode of *Shameless* in January 2019 she admitted that yes, she does feel successful, but later that year she revealed her relationship with success is a little more complicated than she first let on.

'The more the business grows, and the more success I reach, the more I feel like I am not worthy, or I'm not good enough,' Laura confessed to me over a glass of wine. 'The past six months I've battled those feelings more than ever before. Sometimes I feel like an imposter in my own life, like maybe I don't deserve to be here. I spend a lot of time questioning myself, questioning why it was me who got here. The more successful I am, the more I feel that. The higher I climb, the harder the fall could be.'

The passion for work is still incredibly strong, Laura says. Like me, Laura adores what she does. It's just that her work is so closely entwined with a sense of worth – or, on the bad days, worthlessness – that when the validation does come, it can be fleeting.

'The business is doing so well, but in some months we won't have anything new and exciting on, and I'll find myself thinking, "Are we falling behind?" It's almost like everything you've achieved up until that point becomes irrelevant, which is ridiculous.

'One thing I wish I could get rid of is guilt when I'm not working. Even when I'm at uni I feel guilty, which is silly, because I'm still getting a degree and doing something productive! It's so hard not comparing yourself to other people who are running businesses, and feeling like you're lacking in one area or another. There's a lot of guilt, there's a lot of pressure, and not a lot of balance. I don't think people see that, or would know that about running your own business.

'My work does fulfil me. I genuinely love what I do. But at the end of the day, when I think about it, even if we lost everything with the business, I'd still have Dalton, my partner, who loves me. I'd still have my dog, Billy, who just makes every single day better. I'd still have Steph, my best friend. I love working, but those are the things that really matter to me.

'A few years ago, I defined success by having a house, or being on a certain salary, but let me tell you, it's not that at all. Now I define success in my own life by helping people. If I add value to other people's lives, then I think I'm successful.'

At the end of every *Shameless* interview episode, Zara and I ask some of Australia's most successful people how they define success. Despite their numerous accolades, impressive titles and booming social media profiles, only a couple of interviewees have answered with something you could put on a résumé.

Mostly? It's something that's impossible to quantify.

For Lillian Ahenkan, known most commonly as the writer, DJ, television presenter and podcast host FlexMami, success is a continual pursuit of being a better person. It's 'doing things with intention and integrity. Success is not something that you achieve once and then forget about it and move on, success is to keep doing and doing and doing and doing.'

Author, entertainer and broadcaster Em Rusciano says, 'I'm successful if I continue to impact people's lives for the better and leave things better than how I found them, leave people better than how they came. Success for me is people walking out of my show with shiny eyes because they've laughed and cried.'

Professional athlete, motivational speaker, and disability advocate Dylan Alcott defines success as 'making a difference'. Despite winning six consecutive Australian Open Men's Quad Wheelchair Singles titles and a gold medal for wheelchair basketball at the 2008 Paralympics, Alcott believes 'it's not about money or Instagram followers. It's not about grand slams or gold medals – it's about making a difference for my community and the people that I care about. The more famous you get, the more success you have, it's cool, but it's irrelevant to the things that actually matter in life.'

Actress, transgender rights activist and Order of Australia medal recipient Georgie Stone believes 'success is fulfilment . . . it's feeling like you have agency over your life and over your identity. And that can be hard for everyone, for all people, no matter who you are, no matter your gender identity or sexuality. Having agency over your life is something we all have to learn and develop over time, but I feel like success is feeling good in your place, where you are right now, whatever that is to you.'

According to Indigenous activist and writer Marlee Silva, 'It doesn't matter if you're making tons of money. It doesn't matter if you have thousands of followers on Instagram. If you don't feel good about what you're doing every day, it's not success. I'm really lucky in the sense that my success is driven by my passion and the fact that there is nothing in this world that makes me prouder than to be able to say I'm an Aboriginal woman. And, in knowing that every day of my life I'm talking about my culture and championing my people, that's success for me. It doesn't matter that I'm never going to be a millionaire. It's a true honour, and it's exciting and surprising every day.'

Zara and I ask that question because we know that since *Shameless* became A Thing, our own definitions of what does and doesn't constitute success have changed. When the podcast started gaining traction and attracting advertisers, I thought I'd find a sense of satisfaction. When we won the award for Most Popular Podcast at the 2019 Australian Podcast Awards, I thought I'd feel calm. When we landed this book deal, I thought it would be enough. But none of those things brought me any lasting satisfaction. If I were a balloon, they were pumps of helium – a temporary boost until the air seeped out and I felt soft and wrinkly again.

It wasn't until people started using the word 'successful' to describe Zara and me that I realised awards, contracts and sponsorship deals will never make me feel fulfilled. I mean, sure, they're lovely. But they're also hollow and a little lifeless. They populate a LinkedIn page that has no soul. They aren't going to be on my gravestone. They aren't going to be remembered by anyone who actually matters.

Now, I measure my success by the connections I make with other people. If I helped someone feel seen and heard today – if I helped them feel a little less alone, whether that be in my job as a podcaster and writer or just as a human being – then that's a successful day.

In September last year, I went to the funeral of a woman I didn't know very well. She died in her seventies and never had a glittering career. Her life was beautifully ordinary. She filled her time with friends and hobbies. She loved her husband, her children, her grandkids. She made people laugh. She spent most of her days looking sideways, not up.

At her funeral, more than one hundred people basked in the aura she'd left behind. After the service, everyone filed into a sunny room to eat triangle-shaped sandwiches, drink cups of black coffee and chat about their memories of the person who was no longer there to chime in with her sassy quips and anecdotes.

That woman touched more than one hundred people's lives in the time she was alive. On my drive home I thought, *Now, that's success*. If the people eating triangle sandwiches at my funeral look back on my life and say, 'She made me feel welcome,' then I've done my job.

Do I forget this in the rush of the day to day? Of course. I regularly get swept up in the meaningless stuff, like how much I'm earning this month, or our ranking on the Spotify podcast charts. But I also try to debug that pattern of thinking whenever I can.

In my most balanced moments, I feel successful when I make my boyfriend smile. When I take five minutes to give my dog the tummy rub she so desperately craves. When I send an 'I miss you' text to a girlfriend I haven't seen in a while. When I ask, 'Are you okay?' When I say 'I love you' as many times as I think it.

Happiness can be the next rung on the ladder, but it's so much more than that, too. It's falling asleep in the nook where my boyfriend's bicep meets his body. It's listening to Vera Blue. It's Friday night and Saturday morning. It's touching my sister's big, pregnant belly, and feeling a tiny baby kick. It's opening the group chat with my girlfriends to discuss *The Bachelor*. It's noticing the sky on my drive home. It's dancing to my footy team's theme song when the final siren blares. It's the connections we make. The bonds we build. The people we have the privilege of loving.

Most of those things – the great things, the best things – exist outside of my career. They sit quietly in the periphery, sometimes forgotten about when life is enveloped in the chaos of meetings and deadlines. I see them when I look sideways, not up.

Will I keep climbing? Of course. But it's when I pause to look at the view from here that I feel truly alive.

All the things you will learn about yourself and the world when you're on a Euro gap year

- You'll have a Euro boyfriend and confuse it for love. But it's not love. You'd fall in love with anyone right now, given your most taxing daily commitment is deciding what restaurant to visit for dinner. Trust us, whatever 'this' is will end the moment you get on a plane back home. (You might thirstily Snapchat each other for the next four months after that, but that's it, buddy.)

- Personal hygiene. As in, lots of people have none. Like, whatsoever.

- Some hostel managers consider folded sheets in a pillowcase to be a suitable substitute for an *actual pillow*.

- Some hostel managers forget to actually tell you they don't supply linen so, surprise! You'll be using a towel as your blanket tonight, sister.

- Some people will have sex literally anywhere. Including when strangers are around. Including when you are on the bunk bed below them.

- You'll never consider yourself a particularly vengeful person until you sleep in a dorm next to someone who snores louder than those wankers who rev their engines at red lights.

- Some hostels will be populated by creepy dudes who decide to just . . . live there.

- Some people will be halfway across the world, right in front of the most incredible sight, and will still be on their iPhone playing Tetris.

- Cheating is, well, rampant. Lots of guys on your Contiki trip will sleep with everything that moves (including the tour manager) only for you to add them on Facebook on the final day and see they're 'happily' engaged to the 'love of their life'.

- Being lost in the most desolate part of Santorini in forty-five-degree heat with all of your luggage is character-building.

- You realise why people travel with backpacks not suitcases: stairs.

- Speaking of character-building – fuck *Survivor*, 'Keep juuuuust enough money in my bank account so that I never have to call home and ask my sibling if I can borrow $200' is the ultimate game of determination. Outwit, outplay, outlast, little traveller!

- When you stay in a dorm, you learn that some people stay in bed all day. All day.

- Bed bugs are to you what Voldemort was to Harry.

- McDonald's has a remarkable ability to taste different in every country.

- You'll promise to stay in touch with all your new friends – you'll probably even half-plan your next trip together to Canada, or Mongolia, or Mexico – but you'll literally never see each other again.

- . . . and wonder five years later why the fuck you never unfollowed these weirdos on Instagram.

- Lots of people want to steal your shit.

- People will confuse your accent for American.

- Overnight buses and trains will traumatise you forevermore.

- It seems no one actually knows the difference between Australians and Kiwis, either?

- Australia is such a teeny-tiny fish in the grand scheme of things that people will approach you with GENUINE WONDER THAT AN ACTUAL AUSSIE IS IN THEIR MIDST.

- You'll go home and tell people you're different, but . . . you're not, really. You just haven't worked in three months and your brain is feeling like mashed potato.

- There will be times when you feel lonely, and it won't make sense. You can be in the most beautiful, eclectic, colourful place and feel like it is hollow, and that maybe you are too. You went on this trip to have the Time of Your Life. Only, your reality won't always match up with the dream you had in your head, and that's okay.

- You will grow a real affection for homely things: from the way your shower doesn't demand you wear thongs, to how your bed is yours and yours only, to having a fridge with food in it that won't be stolen by strangers. Home is warm. It's nice to be reminded of that.

- You will develop an appreciation for home itself, because no matter where you go, there's a charm to the places and people who made you, you.

- You'll meet people that leave a lasting impression on you, which you'll always be grateful for because you never would have met them in the rigmarole of your typical day-to-day routine.

- You learn that lots of people don't subscribe to a rigid, work-centric model of what life should look like in their twenties. Actually, plenty of wonderful, fulfilled people are more than happy to enrich their days with travel and experiences, not meetings and deadlines. And in connecting with them you will be given the opportunity to consider what you *really* want from your life, free from the prism of your own expectations.

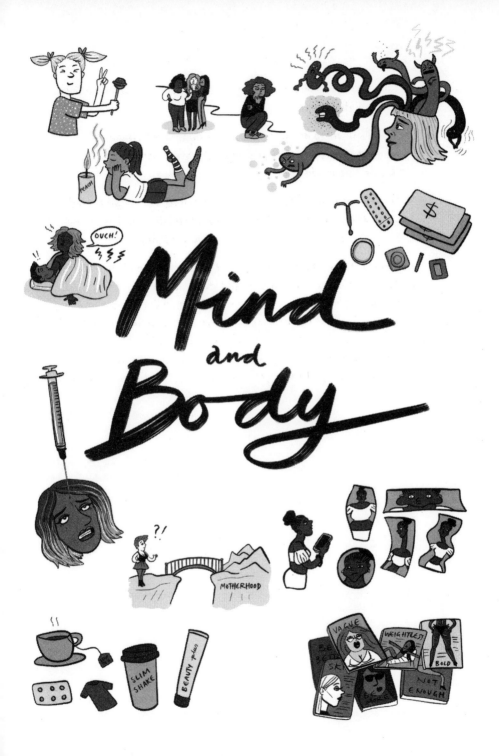

Am I still immature as fuck, or am I a boring adult now?
A checklist

Evidence I am still an overgrown child

☐ I don't have a clue how to pronounce seventy per cent of wine names on any given drinks list, so always resort to asking for 'This one, please' (with my index finger at the ready and a little bit of shame in my wake).

☐ I still *occasionally* get ID'd when buying alcohol.

☐ I flatly refuse to use doorbells. You'll be receiving an 'I'm here' text instead.

☐ Also, I refuse to answer phone calls when I don't recognise the number.

☐ My car will only be serviced every three to three hundred months after the due date because I forgot to budget for it, despite it *being right there* on a sticker in front of my face every day. Of course, I am aware that it will be more expensive the longer I wait, but logic and reason are not my friends.

- [ ] The state of my car is an abomination (wrappers, ev-er-y-where). My wardrobe, too.

- [ ] The dentist. As in, I don't go.

- [ ] I would so much rather pay something off monthly at a more expensive rate than save myself $200 and pay it as a yearly lump sum.

- [ ] I have been to a music festival in the last twelve months.

- [ ] I have also willingly watched an episode of *Keeping Up with the Kardashians*. Okay, fine, I watched an entire season. OKAY FINE I WATCHED THE ENTIRE SERIES.

- [ ] Ironing is not a thing that I do.

- [ ] I have a clock in my apartment that has dead batteries. It has been telling people the incorrect time for over a year now. Is there an easy fix? Yes. Am I the person who's going to fix it? Absolutely not.

- [ ] Sometimes when I'm mid-argument I catch myself saying, 'I'm sorry YOU interpreted it that way.'

- [ ] If my significant other doesn't reply to my text messages within three hours, I will send them a curt 'Okay, coooool' follow-up text.

- [ ] I still don't know what the actual fuck 'negative gearing' is.

- [ ] Ditto 'franking credits'.

- [ ] I will happily spend an hour fake-tanning on Thursday, only to have it slowly deteriorate to a patchy mess by Monday, scrub it off on Tuesday, and repeat the same god-awful cycle again the following week (and repeat until I die, or find . . . better . . . priorities).

- [ ] I am frequently called by my childhood nickname, and know my mum only uses my actual name when I've fucked up.

- [ ] I will consider posting passive-aggressive quotes on my Instagram story after a shitty day at work. I won't actually do it, but I'll think about it. For a long time.

- [ ] And unfollowing you on Instagram is still my ultimate 'fuck you' move.

- [ ] I will spend two hours in bed scrolling on my phone and not consider it to be wasted time.

- [ ] Despite knowing how ludicrously expensive Uber Eats is (and that I really can't afford it) I can't guarantee that tomorrow I won't be swept up in laziness and buy a latte that should cost $4, and a croissant that should cost $8, and spend $24.50 for both to be delivered to my door.

- [ ] I will happily drop too much money on an Asian fusion dinner that didn't even fill me up, but when it comes to spending the same amount on a jumper that will be very practical and keep me warm all winter long? Nah.

- [ ] Swivel chairs on wheels will never not offer profound enjoyment at all times of the day.

- [ ] If I crack my phone screen, you better believe that's just how it's going to be now. It will be cracked for the next two years. Yes, I will continue to complain about it every single day.

☐ My phone charger cord is so frayed from the top that I can only charge my phone at a very specific angle.

☐ I've never quite recovered from the childhood myth that Macca's soft-serve ice cream is made entirely from pig fat.

☐ I've used the same favourite hair tie for the last six months, and don't have a contingency plan for when I lose it.

Evidence I am entering the Dyson vacuum cleaner years

☐ I have a favourite cheese that is brand- and flavour-specific.

☐ I have a quiet but almost desperate desire to go on a health retreat.

☐ I listen to a daily news podcast.

☐ I see a psychologist.

☐ Sometimes on the weekend I rise before 8 am.

☐ The thought of going to a music festival in the next twelve months makes me feel physically ill.

☐ I look at the ages of new *Bachelor* contestants and say, 'Goodness . . . she's a bit . . . young?'

☐ Watching 'acrylic pour' painting videos on YouTube is my porn.

☐ I look at people's artworks and say, 'Oooooh! Whose work is THIS?'

☐ Linen sheets are the best!!!

- [ ] There are . . . bills to pay? And I . . . pay them? On . . . time?
- [ ] Spending my Saturday evening watching *Getaway* doesn't sound like torture.
- [ ] My reflexive response to anyone voluntarily staying out after 1 am is 'Ew'.
- [ ] I watched the rise of apps like 'TikTok' and 'Musical.ly' and thought, *What the actual fuck is this?*
- [ ] I have researched how to remove the mould on my bathroom ceiling on vaguely regressive home maintenance blogs.
- [ ] I have a mildly concerning caffeine addiction and a possibly related sleep problem.
- [ ] The notion of going on a 'digital detox' excites and terrifies me in equal parts.
- [ ] I can't go on a holiday with my partner without our friends spamming the comments section with ring emojis.
- [ ] I have said the phrase 'both things can be true' non-ironically in a debate.
- [ ] Sometimes, I talk about . . . baby names.
- [ ] Remember when Carrie from *Sex and the City* spent $400 on a throw cushion? Yeah. That doesn't sound so absurd to me anymore.
- [ ] Scented candles are now considered a good and worthwhile investment.
- [ ] I've reached the age where fifty per cent of local Instagram influencers are complete strangers to me.

MIND AND BODY

☐ I am easily upset by odd socks and mismatched Tupperware containers.

☐ I understand why my mum always wanted to lie down when we were growing up.

☐ I also understand her rage when we failed to hang the washing on the line while she was at work.

☐ Or defrost that thing from the freezer.

☐ I understand my mum more than I ever thought I would, actually.

The space between one line and two

– MICHELLE –

'So, you missed your pill the day before, or the day after?' my little sister asks as we scan the aisles.

'The day of,' I reply. 'And then I was really late taking it the day after. That's when I realised and took two.'

'*What?*' she says, her eyebrows pushing into her forehead.

'I know. I know it's bad. Why do you think I've spent the last three weeks freaking out?'

We find the tests – all blue and pink and terrifying. As always, they're right beside the condoms – all gold and black and smug.

'So why didn't you use a condom?'

'He doesn't like condoms. No guys like condoms.'

'People who don't like chlamydia like condoms. People who don't like having babies at twenty like condoms. Tell him to get the fuck over it. He's not the one who's going to wind up pregnant.'

She makes a good point. An annoying point, but a very valid one. One I wish I had reiterated to myself three Sundays ago at about 10.30 pm. Condoms would have made this so much easier. You can't forget to use a condom in the same way that you can forget to take a tiny little pill that lives in the back of your wallet. Those things are constantly ducking and dodging my attention. If he had to take a pill every single day without fail – one that caused mood swings, migraines, weight gain and acne – something tells me he'd be clambering to buy *pellets* of condoms. He'd love the things so much he'd fashion them into hats to sell on Etsy.

But, no. His grunts have already made it crystal clear that condoms would be an inconvenience for him. And I don't want to be an inconvenience – the difficult woman who insists on him taking on the tiniest of burdens – so I don't even bother asking anymore.

'How late are you?'

'Six days.'

Six days, but it has felt like double that. For the last week I've been waiting for my period to arrive in all her crampy glory. I've paused in university classes and thought, *That has to be it,* but nope. Nothing. The worst part? I don't even feel like my period is on its way. I'm not bloated, or ravenously hungry, or irritable. I'm not any of the things I typically am right before my period arrives. I'm just scared.

I should have taken the morning-after pill, *I know.* And I would have, only the last time I got it, I felt judgement radiating from the pharmacist's nose-perched glasses and receding hairline. The last time, I spent two hours curled into a ball under my doona. Last time, I told myself there wouldn't be a next time.

And yet, here we are.

'I actually feel pregnant.' My voice shakes a little. 'I just feel like I am. I feel different.'

'Well, let's find out for sure and figure it all out once we know.'

I pick up the cheapest test of the bunch. It doesn't have the digital screen, or any of the fancy add-ons they tell you about in those cheery YouTube ads. It's just a plain old test – one that shows you one line or two.

Fuck.

I shove the box under my arm and walk to the cash register.

Fuck fuck fuck fuck fuck fuck fuck.

A middle-aged woman is working on the checkout and I know she's smiling at me, but I can't lift my eyes to meet hers.

'Hello, just this please,' I mumble, staring at the Butter-Menthols and eucalyptus drops.

'Of course,' she says reassuringly. Beep of the register. Tap my card. Receipt. 'You two have a good day, okay?'

All I can manage is a nod.

Breathe, breathe, breathe.

'Where do you want to do it?' my sister asks quietly as we walk outside into the wind. 'Mum will be home from work by now.'

'Can we do it in there?' I say, pointing to the public toilets. 'I just want to know.'

The tiling on the walls is white and moss-green. With the exception of a toddler and his exasperated mum, we're the only people in the women's cubicles. We walk into the same one, and my sister shuts the door.

I read the instructions. Cap off. Pee on the stick. Make sure you have a constant flow. Cap on. Wait three minutes. Try not to hyperventilate. *Ding ding ding!* Your future awaits, young lady.

I undo the fly on my denim shorts, hold the stick between my legs and wait. I place the test on top of the toilet paper dispenser and start the timer on my phone.

My sister is talking about exam preparations to distract me, but I'm already gone. I'm gone, thinking about what the fuck happens next, about how much my life could change in three minutes' time. I'll get an abortion, right? *Right?* How much do abortions even cost? Are they covered by Medicare? If they're expensive,

I'm kind of screwed, but maybe I could ask my best friend for a loan. And what about him? How do you tell a boy – a boy who isn't even your boyfriend – that you're pregnant with his child? Do I tell him at all? No, I'd have to. It's his, too. I wonder if he'd come with me and hold my hand. I wonder if he'd feel sad, or angry, or nothing at all. I wonder if the procedure would hurt, and how I'd hide the recovery from my parents.

Or could I do this parenting thing alone? Stranger things have happened. So many women have done this alone, and I might be young but I'm strong. I'm not ready, but I'd make a good mum. Mum and Dad would be shocked at first and maybe a little disappointed, but pretty quickly they'd be over the moon. I know they'd be hands-on. Dad has wanted grandchildren since the day we turned eighteen, so maybe they'd want this for me. Maybe I could do it.

But.

I know, deep down, that I'd be doing this without a partner. He'd leave. I'd never see him again. I'd be a single mum. A mum to a living, breathing baby. A baby. One that might be inside of me, right now. I could defer uni for a few years – until the child is in kindergarten, maybe – and finish my degree later. But would I? Would I go back, or would this throw everything I've planned off course? And what about money? Nappies are expensive and I have $156 to my name. Would this set us up for a life of hardship? What about my body? Will it stretch and sag? What about dating? How many twentysomething guys want to date a single mum? What if I met the right guy – The Guy – in a few years' time, but my situation scared him away?

My alarm is ringing. I see my face mirrored in my sister's, who is standing with her back against the door. At least she'll be with me, no matter what, whether we're in a clinic or a labour ward.

I lean over.

One faint, pink line.

Not two, just one.

I'm relieved. Relieved and . . . angry?

Because it's not really just one line. It's one line and six long days of mental gymnastics – of flipping and contorting and spinning and fretting – because contraception is something that's put onto me and me alone.

Why? Because apparently this is *my* problem, *my* domain, something for me to handle, all while ensuring it never dints his experience, his pleasure. He doesn't want to know about it, you see. Oh, but did he mention that he *really hates condoms*? That's the only bit he truly cares about. He'll remind me about that part often. The rest of it – the research and the appointments and the cash and the daily reminders and the many, many side effects? That's on me.

And so, there's one little line. I'm not pregnant. Breathe. It's okay. Everything will be okay.

Only, I can't help but feel that something about this just isn't fair. That he's at home playing PlayStation, and I'm here. That today and tomorrow and next month I'll be expected to Have It Under Control, while the invisible pressure to not ask anything of him makes me feel totally powerless.

I can already hear him asking 'Why do I have to wear a condom? You're on the Pill, aren't you?'

I can already see the next pharmacist's sneer.

The next cashier's careful nod.

The next bathroom.

The next test.

And I just know that this won't be the last time that I'm made to carry the full weight of something that's supposed to be shared.

The space between what we are told about sex and how it is for me

– ZARA –

I don't actually remember the first time I tried to have sex. I don't remember the second, third or fourth times either. The times after that are a faceless blur, a mess of pain, distress and self-loathing. I wonder now if I felt so much shame and anxiety that my memories obstructed themselves, shrouding those moments in a haze so that I never had to relive them again.

All I can tell you about the first time I tried to have sex is that I was seventeen, and in the months after, I thought my body was broken, or that it was wired differently, or that its internal functions were forever flawed. By the time I was eighteen, I had resigned myself to the fact that having sex meant I'd always feel like I was being attacked from the inside, and that the only cure for the sharp, shooting pain was not having sex at all.

It took a year for me to recognise things weren't normal, and even longer than that to tell a doctor that something wasn't right. It is vaginismus, my gynaecologist told me at age nineteen, a condition that saw my muscles involuntarily contract to such a degree that sex was either painful or impossible. It is vaginismus and we will fix it, she told me once more, but what transpired instead was a stretch of seven years I spent hating myself, struggling to find a meaningful way to heal. A time I felt tortured by loneliness, suffocated by shame and convinced I would never find love, so long as my insides remained this scarred.

I was a magazine junkie as a kid. I dreamed of being a writer, of having my words grace the pages of the glossy magazines I read so aggressively that the corners of each cover would turn inwards and the binding would begin to break. It began with *Total Girl*, *Girlfriend* and then *Dolly* with its elusive sealed section, brimming with stories about sex and relationships that I read but never quite understood. By fifteen I had graduated to *Cosmopolitan*, a magazine that sold itself on sex, its monthly cover never complete without SEX capitalised in the top left corner, accompanied by its usual rotation of tips, questions and stories about heteronormative, penetrative sex.

Before I even knew how to have sex, I was saturated with messages about it: sex would happen, it would likely happen soon, I would know what to do when it did and of course, that I would enjoy every part of it. The latter seemed like a foregone conclusion, a fact of teenage existence: it might be awkward to start with, but eventually sex would become a central part of my identity, my conversations with my girlfriends and a relationship I wasn't yet in.

At seventeen, when I found myself in a relationship and ready to have sex, I tried to reconcile everything I thought I knew about sex with the way I was actually experiencing it. Some days, sex felt like knuckles colliding with a brick wall as my muscles knitted tightly together, involuntarily contracting in the very moments I begged them not to. Other times, it felt like someone was inserting a knife inside me – an agonising measure of my already floundering pain threshold.

I would feel bruised in the moments after, my mind despising my body for the things it had failed to do, and my body despising my mind for being the one to put myself through it. So that he who was lying next to me would not notice my tears, I would drag myself to the bathroom and sit my bare skin on the ground, the biting cold of the floor tiles a distraction from the anger swallowing my mind.

My partner at the time was patient and kind, promising me it was something we never had to do and pain I should never have to experience. But despite his best assurances, there was little he could do to rewrite a decade of messages I had internalised about sex and relationships: sex was something you owed your partner, an activity men inherently needed to stay sane and a relationship without it was destined to die.

So, sex became a chore: one that made my chest tighten and my eyes sting, my heart hurt and my soul sink. But I needed it, and I needed it badly because without it, no one would think my relationship was real. And if people didn't think my relationship was real, did it actually mean anything at all?

When I was eighteen and at schoolies, I have this distinct memory of being cornered in the bathroom of a Byron Bay bar by three of my very tipsy, very giggly best friends.

'Have you had sex?' they asked me with a sly smile. 'Why wouldn't you just tell us if you *have* had sex?'

I was the cagey friend, the one who held her stories close to her chest and kept her worries confined to her mind. They couldn't understand why I didn't want to bond with them over awkward mishaps, clumsy foreplay and teenage boys who had egos bigger than their abilities. I considered telling them the truth: that I hated sex, perhaps more than I hated anything else. I could have told them how embarrassed I was, how dark my thoughts were becoming, how overwhelming the isolation was. How I felt trapped in a lair I did not know how to climb out of.

But instead I laughed and let them assume I hadn't yet, because my shame assured me it was easier than telling them the story on the tip of my tongue.

At nineteen, in the months after I was diagnosed with vaginismus, I did not tell my friends, my sister or my parents. My then-boyfriend knew, but even then, I'm not sure I ever gave him the words or the tools to move through it by my side. I found myself in a dark and deep state of denial, hoping that if I ignored the hold it had on my mind, perhaps it would loosen its clutches on my self-esteem. Eventually, I drip-fed the people close to me enough details to communicate that things weren't okay, but not enough for them to know how to meaningfully and adequately help me.

I refused to seek out stories of women who were like me. I did not Google the condition to find articles that could have provided comfort because I was terrified of acknowledging that their reality was my own. As luck would have it, vaginismus had such little airtime in the public sphere that it was possible to avoid them entirely. At the time I thought this was a silver lining: at least I wasn't involuntarily reminded of vaginismus when I opened Facebook, Instagram or wanted to read an article on any of my favourite news websites. It wasn't until much later that I recognised that that 'silver lining' was the most claustrophobic prison of all. All it meant was that when I was eventually faced with stories of women like me, they would undo me in a way I had not yet prepared my mind for.

At twenty-one, when I worked in women's media as a casual writer, I remember being scheduled to work on a Saturday. Mich and I were both rostered on as the junior content producers that day but we worked our respective shifts from home. In the early afternoon, our editor published a story by an American writer called Lara Parker. Our editor had been holding on to the story for a time in the day when traffic on the website was dropping and our numbers desperately needed a boost. I caught the headline and nearly choked on the lukewarm cup of green tea at my lips.

'What it's like to date when you can't have sex.'

I clicked into the story and skimmed the copy. Parker, too, had vaginismus. Parker, too, was dogged with confusion and shame, articulating her inability to properly explain to the men she was dating why her body never cooperated with her desire.

I remember jumping out of the story and opening a program called Chartbeat, a tool some news organisations use to track how many people are reading a story at any given time. The story was being read by twenty times more people than any other story on the site. Meanwhile, Slack was alive with relief and elation and excitement from everyone in the team working that Saturday. Our traffic for the day was back on track.

I felt betrayed in the most irrational way possible: by an oblivious editor who knew a story as unique as this one would drive traffic, and by every person who clicked in a frenzy. I felt like the internet's plaything; today's clickbait freak show.

I worked through the rest of my shift and closed my laptop, making the metres-long journey from my desk to my bed when the clock struck 5 pm. I crawled into a ball and held my knees so close to my chest, my tears tumbled onto my shins rather than pooling on my cheeks.

Perhaps now, I told myself between sobs, perhaps now is the time to properly fix it.

Here's what you're not told when you seek treatment for chronic pain: first, it's really fucking expensive and second, in order to fix it, you have to inflict on yourself the very pain you're doing everything to avoid.

From the moment a doctor gave me a vaginismus diagnosis, I made an effort to do everything I could to get it fixed. It should take a matter of months, my doctor told me. She referred me to a pelvic floor physiotherapist who was young, sporty and well accustomed to the issues I brought to her. We made a remarkable effort to commit to surface-level small talk as she inserted various tools up my vagina, finding a way to cover overseas travel or her marathon training while politely ignoring the fact she now had intimate insight into the most broken parts of my body.

If being unable to have sex was a mindfuck, then the cycle of trying to fix it was a shambles of its own kind. I would pay for each appointment at reception and meekly text my mother, asking if perhaps I could borrow $50 again because I had another medical consultation and now I had no money for the rest of the week. She would rubbish my half-hearted promises to pay her back, saying she wanted to help me fix my condition, and if that meant paying for any and all of my appointments then *hell*, she would learn how to use internet banking. That's what you don't hear about chronic pain and the economics of healing: fixing it takes an inestimable stretch of time and a bunch of expensive appointments. If I had not been able to text my mother and sheepishly ask for financial help, what hope would I have had in paying for the treatment I needed?

I would leave each appointment with high spirits and higher hopes; my physiotherapist's assurances that it would get better beaming small rays of sunshine onto an overcast, cloudy mind. With an A4 sheet of exercises folded haphazardly in my wallet, I would head home, sit quietly in my bedroom and follow her instructions. The idea was to sit through the pain: each exercise encouraged me to push through the discomfort until my muscles had stopped their reflexive spasms. Instead of noting down progress, I would count down until it was over because every shooting, knife-like sensation would remind me of the agony I was trying to numb, meaning every shooting, knife-like sensation would remind me of how worthless it all made me feel.

Let's take a day off from the exercises tomorrow, I'd promise both my body and my mind – but one day would turn into two, and two into seven, and a week into a month where I'd stopped treatment again. But of course, there's only so long you can dawdle behind your own truth: eventually, something would remind me of how much I hated my own reality and so I'd book back in with my physiotherapist, ready for Groundhog Day, ready to go through the motions all over again.

Over the course of the seven years I sought treatment for vaginismus I visited a physiotherapist, two gynaecologists, another doctor to talk about the potential of botox as a form of treatment, a sexual therapist and countless GPs to seek out a new treatment none of them actually knew how to prescribe. All were time-consuming, emotionally taxing and expensive. I now look back and wonder if my first port of call should have always been a psychologist.

∼

On an uncharacteristically warm Thursday in April 2019, I went for a run by the beach. The day had been full of interviews for *Love Etc.*, a podcast about sex and relationships we were producing on behalf of Bumble Australia. One of the interviews we had conducted earlier that day was with Chantelle Otten, a sex therapist who was our expert voice in an episode on conditions that made sex painful. I told Michelle I wanted desperately to include in the series an episode on conditions like vaginismus, but didn't think I could put my voice to it. She kindly agreed, and kindly told me there was no story I ever had to tell for the sake of good content.

My running track – on the times when, you know, I can *actually be bothered to exercise* – is one of the only places in the world that can clear my cluttered mind. It has the ocean on one side and shrubbery on the other, a suburban cocoon of dirt track, giving you the illusion you are far from the chaos you're likely running from. I may have been only a kilometre in when I stopped running and called Mich. I was crying, I think, but not audibly enough for her to notice.

I told her I needed to do the episode, that I couldn't possibly produce a podcast series leveraging the courage of other women's stories while not being strong enough to tell my own. She asked me more than a handful of times if I was sure, if I would regret being so open, if it would stir up some thoughts and feelings I had not properly dealt with. I told her I was sure, that I didn't want to edit the episode or ever listen back to it, but that we could record the following week. We decided to put eight weeks between recording the interview and it going live.

It's a funny thing, sitting down with one of your closest friends to talk about something that has dogged you intimately for the better part of six or seven years and having her knowing nothing about it. She was gentle with me, like I knew she always would be. Recording with her felt scary and stressful but safe. I told her everything I had been too terrified to admit to myself: that now I was single, I wasn't sure how I would ever be loved. How, now I was talking about it, I worried I would always be branded as the girl who couldn't have sex.

The afternoon I went running and decided, through streams of public tears, that I should finally talk, I didn't expect that every corner of my mind would start to relax. That, in forcing myself to talk to thousands of strangers, I would be forcing myself to finally talk to my parents, my girlfriends and my new friends. That in opening up, I would finally be letting myself breathe. The minute I left that recording session, the cloud of self-loathing and guilt and shame I had buried myself under began to dissipate.

Two weeks before we published the episode, I met Oli, the person who would soon become my boyfriend and the best person I have ever met. I had known him for little more than a week when I asked for his email address and sent him the edited recording. I felt exposed – stupidly so, but I figured this time, and with this person, I would be open. He would know what vaginismus was and why it had asphyxiated my mind and eroded my self-confidence for so long. He wrapped me up in his gentleness, in his generosity, in his well-attuned and acute understanding of how much I had just laid bare. For the first time in my life I decided to use my words, and they landed on a cushion of kindness.

In the days and weeks after that episode went live, I was inundated with other women's stories: stories I had spent so long trying to avoid. They were stories from women in silos. Women who were in pain and didn't know why, women who didn't know how to tell their friends and their parents or, in some cases, their partner. Women who didn't know what help to get or where to even find it. Women who were at a loss as to why sex wasn't what the world told them it was going to be.

In the same way I used to avoid stories about vaginismus, I used to avoid people who told me how easy it was to fix. I resented them, and I resented them hugely. I resented the inference that my inability to heal was because I didn't want it enough, and the implication that chronic pain was in my head, and all I needed to do was relax.

Irrationally, I resented, too, the people who had fixed theirs. *I've been working at this for six years. Why isn't it my turn to get better?*

One of the hardest parts of telling this story is the knowledge that, had I read my own story six years ago, I would have resented myself, too. I would have begrudged reading that my body started to heal the minute I began to forgive it. I would have struggled to accept that sex stopped being painful when I stopped feeling so much shame about it, or when I finally had the words to talk about it. I would've hated the neat bow, the happy ending, the convenient end to a complicated tale.

But I cannot write you a different ending. I can only tell you that vaginismus loosened its clutches on my mind when I started to let people in, when I refused to feel shame and when I realised there were thousands of young women across Australia suffering in the silence of their dark bedrooms and in the depths of their darker minds.

In the six or so years in which I sought treatment, I remember the countless times my doctors told me to relax, to have a couple of drinks before having sex because that would surely loosen me up. They never told me in as many words, but I always got the sense they thought I was stuck in my own head a little too much. That if I just let myself breathe, I would heal in a way I'd been desperate to for so long.

They were right, but perhaps not in the way they intended: I *was* stuck in my own head. I was trapped there, a victim of our narrow-minded and isolating public conversations about sex. I was buried in a burrow of shame and embarrassment, denial and self-loathing. I was buried there, because no one told me there was a path to get out.

I don't remember the first time I ever tried to have sex. Instead, I remember the first time I tried to start talking about it.

29 things only people with anxiety will understand

1. Fights with your significant other because you've asked 'What's wrong?' so many times in quick succession that asking 'What's wrong?' is *precisely what's fucking wrong.*

2. The sheer panic that descends when you see a full stop at the end of an otherwise ordinary text message.

3. The mandatory three-hour cool-off period between receiving a confrontational email and actually gathering the strength to read it and reply.

4. Mentally writing your sister's obituary when she doesn't reply to your texts for two hours and has therefore definitely died in a car accident.

5. Filing that obituary away with the ones you've written for your boyfriend, dad and second cousin Jemima once you realise your sister is very much alive and simply dared to take a nap.

6. Starting sentences with, 'I know this is just my anxiety talking, but ...'

7. Responding to logic and reason with, 'I KNOW IT DOESN'T MAKE SENSE.'

8. Apologising for anxiety-fuelled outbursts with, 'I will get better at controlling this stuff, I promise.'

9. The dread of an airport security queue, where you need to empty every aerosol can, rogue perfume bottle and your laptop into blue tubs in militant fashion (without being an inconvenience to all the very busy and important-looking strangers behind you).

10. Seeing the price tag on an anxiety blanket and thinking, *Worth it.*

11. Feeling personally offended by anyone who believes that horror movies are a form of 'entertainment'.

12. Accepting an invite for a night out drinking wine, knowing Future You is going to despise Present You for it.

13. Looking at your fifth glass and wondering, *Will this be the one that catapults me into a panic attack?*

14. The dawning realisation that, yes, that was the glass. FUN!

15. The extra-terrestrial level of shitness when your wine hangover is coupled with a panic attack hangover.

16. The freedom of taking your first deep breath post-panic attack.

17. The pre-psychologist-appointment anxiety spike.

18. The post-psychologist-appointment food binge (because you just cried out half your body weight in tears and have earned it).

19. Convincing yourself you failed that exam, even though you're a good student who did more than enough study and answered every question in full.

20. Convincing yourself you're going to return a positive drug test after being pulled over at a booze bus, even though you haven't smoked weed since 2017.

21. Deciding you're the most annoying person on the planet every five to seven business days.

22. Flaking out of social engagements because the thought of not knowing what to say in conversation or – even worse – *not having anyone to talk to at all* makes you want to cry.

23. Having flashbacks of something you said three years ago and spontaneously shuddering.

24. Developing a fear that your boss thinks you're incompetent.

25. Developing a fear that your mum thinks you're stuck up.

26. Developing a fear that your friends think you're bitchy.

27. Having a grandparent who calls you a 'worrywart', but is always on hand with biscuits and tea when the moment calls for it.

28. Having a golden co-worker who understands that you can't work right now, and quietly picks up that task while you have a cry.

29. Having a girlfriend who you tag in anxiety memes because as shitty as this illness is, and as close to death as it sometimes makes you feel, it also connects you to some pretty remarkable women. Women who have Been There, who Get It, and by extension get you too.

The space between my personality and my mental illness

— MICHELLE —

Let me set the scene of my most vivid childhood memory:

I am five, and at the park with my family. My siblings are playing near a miniature bridge that's overlooking a lake. My baby brother Tom is just beginning to walk and while my parents prepare our lunches, he takes a particular interest in the ducks. He toddles up to the bridge and peers over the edge, cooing at the water and at all the animals the light unearths.

It should be a gentle, pastel-coloured childhood memory. Nothing untoward happened, and judging by my mum's 'vague recollection' of the day, it was a perfectly lovely family lunch in the park. Only, when I think back to my little brother in his overalls, giggling at the ducks, I feel sick. Because that day wasn't a pleasant or calming outing for me. Actually, it was a day when I felt desperation and panic. I saw my gorgeous little brother, with his blond hair and button nose, approach the bridge again and again. I saw his eyes widen at the birds, his tiny hand stretch out to offer them clumps of bread. I saw how fascinated he was by his reflection in the water, how he tilted his little body towards it. I saw something that neither of my parents did: Tom was going to topple over the edge.

He was going to die. He was going to die and I was convinced nobody else saw that possibility – that *probability* – except me.

I watched Tom like a hawk that day. I felt my heart batter in my chest whenever I lost sight of him, even just for a second. Wherever he went, I went, for the entire afternoon, furious that my parents could eat ham and cheese sandwiches two metres away when catastrophe was all but certain.

Only, it wasn't. The day went on, we ate our sandwiches, we packed up, and climbed into our hulking grey-blue Toyota Tarago. Tom was fine. He remains more than fine to this day; I'm happy to report he grew into a six-foot-seven man with a slightly weaker interest in pond flora and fauna.

The panic, though? That stuck around.

As I grew older, my fear only grew, too.

I've always been a 'worrier'. As a kid, adults regularly told me so.

'You're such a worrywart,' they'd laugh, rubbing my hair, patting my shoulders, kissing my forehead. 'You're always fretting about something!'

Worrying is such a familiar state of being to me that it feels enmeshed with being alive. Concerns and qualms eke their way into almost every conversation I have, slithering out indiscriminately, as if there's no topic that's quarantined from a little panic, a dollop of stress.

My mum has always mused that I am the way I am because of her. Mum fell pregnant with me when she was still navigating the all-consuming loss of my sister, Jennifer, who was born sleeping.

Mum was so grief-stricken when I was in her belly – so terrified that she would lose me, too – that she recalls her pregnancy with me as the most worrying time of her life. There wasn't a morning she woke without anxiety. Not until she held my skinny, wriggly body in her arms did she allow herself to take a deep breath and consider her future with a second child. She tells me this story over cups of tea whenever I'm having a particularly anxious day, as if she's apologising for something that was entirely outside of her control.

'You're that way because of me,' she says, convinced that her anxiety had travelled through the placenta.

My dad has always described me as 'sensitive'. I *feel* a lot, and often. 'You wear your heart on your sleeve, sweetheart,' he would tell me when I was a child. 'It's beautiful.'

My siblings mostly giggle when I choose to fret about something particularly niche, like the possibility that I have emphysema, despite being in my twenties . . . *with zero smoking history.*

My friends call me a 'stress head'. I was that annoying student in the corridor after a psychology exam asking things like, 'WHAT DID YOU GET FOR QUESTION ELEVEN?' I'd then proceed to toss in my bed at night, reflecting on question eleven and how I totally fucked it up in every conceivable way and how it would singlehandedly unravel my life. Upon receiving my results a few weeks later, I'd be genuinely surprised – I'd performed well, *particularly on question eleven.* Then I'd have a maths test the next morning, develop a deep panic over question twenty-three and repeat the same inglorious cycle. My friends would groan and say that this time would be just like the last, and that I was overreacting, to which I'd positively insist that, No, this time I was serious, and I was going to fail school, drop out and become someone involved in a neighbourly dispute on *A Current Affair.*

This kind of anxiousness was manageable, though. I was a little irritating to be near after a test, sure, but on the whole I was a normal teenager. Only, as I grew older – and had negative experiences that deviated from my idyllic middle-class upbringing in the suburbs – my anxiety bubbled up and spilled over, staining everything in my existence a pale red.

When I hit my twenties, it wasn't just a matter of stressing about uni results, or wanting to excel at work. It wasn't just perfectionism, or protectiveness over the people I love. It became something darker, something debilitating. The metamorphosis of a personality trait that had long defined me didn't produce a butterfly. It produced a snake that had wrapped itself around my neck.

I first realised something was wrong with my mind when travelling to work became exhausting. I was twenty-three, the weekend editor at Mamamia at the time, and my trip into the office was a straightforward one. I'd catch a tram into the city, then I'd walk through Melbourne Central Shopping Centre and into work. It was an easy commute, during which I could basically chill out and listen to a podcast.

And yet, as if overnight, I found I couldn't walk down my own street without checking over my shoulder every few steps, convinced that a mysterious man would be lingering nearby. I crossed the road cautiously, concerned that a speeding car might wipe me out if I wasn't careful. I flinched when a stranger brushed past me as they made their way to the Myki readers. The odd characters that make St Kilda what it is – the colourful people of the city I love – now terrified me. I met their eyes with damp, sweaty fear. If someone with a backpack walked onto the tram, my stomach turned into a blender. *They're a terrorist*, my mind decided. *That man is a terrorist and he has a bomb in that backpack.* A podcast episode was now a distraction, something that could pull my attention away from the likely terrorist sitting four seats down. *And if that guy isn't a terrorist, then I bet the one down the other end of the carriage staring back at me certainly is.*

The urge to take flight became so strong that I would swap trams upon seeing anyone who looked remotely dodgy. I would get off at the next stop, only to realise another dodgy guy would be on this tram, too, and now I'd be ten minutes late to work. The task of walking through the shopping centre was another mission entirely; I jogged through the crowds, ducking and dodging passers-by as if a bomb would detonate us all to smithereens at any moment.

Every day for six weeks, I felt like I was under siege. It was 2017 and the world seemed cold in the shadow of the May bombings at Ariana Grande's Manchester concert. In the preceding weeks I had covered the story at length. If I wasn't commissioning articles about what happened to those young people – most of them girls – I was collating lists of the victims, trying to squeeze their stories into sentences, cropping their smiley Instagram selfies to fit the website's desired dimensions. I was waiting for the next name, the next family statement, the next human horror story to unfold. I was researching the bomber's upbringing and wondering how a human being could be so corrupt and vile.

Then, in June, the London Bridge attack seized the news cycle. I was again tasked with editorial coverage; it was my job to know the blow-by-blow account of what those three men did with that van and their knives. I studied the second-by-second accounts of what happened to the eight victims. Every horrific detail seeped into my brain. The chances of being killed by a machete blade or nail bomb didn't seem minuscule anymore. It seemed inevitable.

I could no longer imagine a world in which I or someone I loved wouldn't become the victim of a terrorist attack.

The more terror became entwined with my work, the more I gravitated towards true crime content in my downtime. I wanted to know how serial killers set about raping and murdering women. I wanted to understand the minds of evil psychopaths who drove their cars into groups of people. I wanted to familiarise myself with the behavioural patterns, the rationales, the mental processes of wanting to kill someone. The more I knew about what happened to victims, I figured, the more I could protect myself and the people I love. It was the last thing my anxiety-addled mind needed, but it also felt like self-preservation.

Most days, upon arriving at the office I would crumple into a soggy mess of sweat, snot and tears. After one particularly unsettling tram ride, the anxiety was so ferocious I couldn't even look at my laptop screen. I was so positively filled with fear that I could not stop crying; I moved myself to a table by the kitchen and let the tears stream down my face for two hours, pausing only to accept a fresh cup of tea from Zara, who had grown concerned after noticing the racket of keyboard tapping and phones ringing was punctuated by my sniffles and sobs.

The way I described my panic attacks to Zara that day – and the way I've found most helpful ever since – is that they're like a gushing tap. It takes a daily conscious effort to tighten the valves of an anxious and unreasonable mind. You've let drips out here and there, but suddenly the pressure has risen so much it feels like a tsunami is brewing. You can try to rationalise with the least rational part of your brain – try to convince yourself that everything is fine, that you're going to be okay, that this is just anxiety again. But then the tap bursts open, and the water is gushing out, and you can't lift your head above the water, let alone try to swim against the current. The negative self-talk is cascading. That logical part of you is still there, somewhere, but the force of the water is too great for you to find her. She's drowned out by the screams of your odious fears. *You're annoying, nobody likes you, you can't breathe, you're ugly, you're stupid, you're going to die.* You know that there's nothing you can do, and so you acquiesce. You turn onto your back and let the toxic water come and come and come, as you try to float your way through. You let the self-hatred wash over you, wet your hair, drip from your eyelashes, pool in your bellybutton. You let it flood into every nook and cranny of your weak body. You are at your lowest ebb. You have unlocked your most broken self, but you are still alive. Your chest is still billowing with new oxygen, new life, new moments, new thoughts.

It might take thirty minutes, it might take a full day, but eventually you realise that your inner self is a stronger swimmer than you gave her credit for, because she's managed to wrangle the tap and force those valves shut again.

The sun comes out.

You're in the clear again.

What surprised me most in the early days of my anxiety disorder is that my panic attacks were characterised by feelings of self-hatred, not nervousness. Mid-panic attack, I hated myself so viscerally that telling you about it now makes me wince in pain. In my worst moments, I said things to myself that I never want to repeat. The hatred became so intense that it made me want to flee my own body. I wanted to escape, although to where I was never quite sure. The tidal wave of self-hatred saw me break things methodically, maniacally. I've smashed plastic coathangers, one by one, against my wooden bed frame. I've thrown glasses on the floor, just for the release of seeing something shatter. I've screamed into pillows and down hallways, desperate to let all the brokenness out of my throat. I despise myself in these moments. I convince myself that the world despises me, too.

Sometimes my anxiety disorder makes me feel injured. I feel like I've failed some prefatory life test, that I am incapable of navigating the everyday hurdles that others bound over without drawing breath. When my mind isn't terrified of strange men murdering me, it's terrified that perhaps other people are busy living while I am holding my head in my hands because the world suddenly appears as if it's made of Aeroplane Jelly.

I wish my skin was a little thicker. I wish I didn't need thirty minutes to compose myself before opening daunting emails in my inbox. I wish I didn't go through stages of becoming convinced that I have emphysema, or alopecia, or leukaemia. I wish I could approach life with the gung-ho zest of someone who faces her fears with a smile. I wish I could wish the anxiety away.

My anxiety has on occasion been a source of tension in my relationship. It has held me back from social events, difficult conversations, confronting news reports and packed trams. It has held me back from the grit that makes life ugly and real.

But I don't hate my anxiety, either. As much as it torments my mind now and then, it also makes me who I am. It makes me decent at my job because I care deeply about the work I produce. It makes me passionate about the world I live in, because I want to help others where I can and give back in some small way. It makes me a good girlfriend, sister, daughter and friend because I am attentive to how my loved ones are doing.

I love a lot and I love deeply. I say so at the end of every phone call, happy birthday message and long day. If I love somebody, I don't want them to ever spend a second doubting it. Sometimes I'll tell Mitch five times in an hour, until he looks up from his dinner plate and says, 'Yes, Mich, I think you might have told me that already. And I love you too.'

The beauty of my job is that Zara and I get to meet so many incredible women for our 'In Conversation' episodes and call it Thursday. The businesswomen, authors and media personalities we sit down with are leaders and game-changers. While their walks of life can be worlds apart, each possesses unwavering drive: a trait that threads their stories together in a tapestry of female kickarsery.

Ironically, many are bound together by another thread, too: anxiety. It turns out that when you spend an hour with some of Australia's most influential women, you learn many of them are trying to tranquilise a monster that's squatting in the kinetic contours of their brains. It seems so incongruous, but being wildly likeable and talented while having a mental illness that convinces you that you're hated and hopeless is the case for so many. If anything, the *Shameless* interviewees have shown us that the higher you climb, the more agitated the monsters of self-doubt and fear can get.

When we asked bestselling author and comedian Tanya Hennessy to reflect on how her steep career trajectory affected her anxiety, she said, '[The self-doubt] absolutely got louder. It's still really loud. I still see a psych. I see a kinesiologist. You name someone with a crystal and I'll be having a chat with them ... I talk to my friends a lot about it, but making stuff makes me happy and that's what I come back to every time. Just keep making stuff.'

For radio host Ash London, who experienced an anxiety disorder in her late twenties, the trappings of a career in the public eye can also include a level of pressure and scrutiny that isn't healthy for the mind.

'I get heart palpitations if I feel like something I've said might be taken out of context,' Ash said. 'I will ruminate over it for days . . . I hate flying and I find it really hard to get on a plane. I fly a lot, and every second that I'm on a flight I'm anxious. [My anxiety] rears its ugly, disgusting, despicable head up in many ways, but I see a psychologist. I'm doing all the things I have to do to keep my head above the water . . . there are just moments when I feel things are slipping out of my control.'

For author and former lawyer Georgie Dent, who wrote her book *Breaking Badly* about having a breakdown in her twenties, there is no clear distinction between her personality and her mental illness: both things bleed into each other.

'One psychologist once said to me, "You've got to think about all of the parts of your personality that make you you." It's recognising what the toxic components of my anxiety are, putting those things in check and saying, "I am an anxious person. I'll always be an anxious person. And I'm okay with accepting those parts of my personality."'

Therein lies the conundrum: if I've always been an anxious person, how can I know where the illness ends and my personality begins? To eliminate the anxious parts of myself would be to change the make-up of who I am.

This doesn't mean I'll tell my psychologist her work is done and stop going to therapy. This is still an illness that needs to be managed. To stop attending my sessions would be akin to binning my asthma inhalers, or refusing to take antibiotics for an infection. Since seeing my psychologist, I've gone from being so terrified of life that I wouldn't wear heels in public because they might inhibit me from running away from a suicide bomber, to living relatively free from doom and gloom. I have barely listened to a true-crime podcast or watched a murder mystery in the past three years. I no longer fill my brain with gruesome content as a means of self-preservation. I can sit on a packed tram without worrying that it's going to blow up.

There are bad days, of course, but now they are merely the pepper on what is a pretty amazing life. I see my psychologist every six weeks, and the routine we have set together seems to be working. Anxiety does pop up in some form every week, if not every day, but it's not the kind that makes me feel like I'm drowning. It's a trickle of water, one that reminds me that this is just how I am. I am sensitive. I am prone to feelings of apprehension and stress. I am malleable and fallible. But there is strength in admitting that you're not okay and seeking help to get better. There is strength in observing the world around you. There is strength in feeling things and feeling them fully. There is strength in being diligent, thoughtful, passionate, emotional. There is strength in anxiety, because it shows just how much you care.

Is my anxiety an illness? Yes. But in some ways it is also my unique superpower, one that allows me to pour love into the humans and things around me. Sometimes it's a superpower that hurts me. It's one that has inflicted pain and torment. But it's also one that makes me, well, me.

Society loves trying to define the boundaries of what is and isn't mental illness. We invent diagnostic tools, we pore over medical manuals with a fine-toothed comb, we tweak labels and words and phrases so that the boundaries of what constitutes a personality trait and what constitutes sickness are kept as clearly defined as possible. We want to be able to point to mental illness like it's a tangible thing; like we can hold it and mould it however we see fit. Like either it is there, or it isn't. But, sometimes, trying to cage mental illness is like trying to cage smoke. The anxiety monsters of my brain can't be stunned with tranquiliser guns because they are amorphous.

I've learned that I can't kill the monsters. But I can coax and tame them instead. And once they're tame? I embrace them as my neighbours. Neighbours that might always be there, but who make my mind a colourful apartment building – a place I've grown to love for all the cracks in the walls and the incandescent glow that shines through them.

The space between my body, my fertility and my future

– ZARA –

Some days – most days, in fact – I do this thing where I imagine my life in two, five, sometimes ten years' time. I think about the person I'll be. Will I laugh more, or less? Will I be hardened, or gentler? Will the world have been kind to me, or will it have dealt its blows? I think about the people who will be around me and the ones who might fall away. I think about my career and my hobbies and my happiness, and wonder how they will intersect with each other. I think about my purpose. Will work continue to drive me so intensely, or will I have settled on that front? I think about my identity. I think about the kinds of things that will change and how deeply I might be shaken by a new reality.

And I wonder, often, whether I'll have kids by a certain point. I consider all the different points along my personal timeline at which I could become a mother, and the forces in my life – be it work, finances or love – that would help or hinder that pursuit. Will it be Then? And if not Exactly Then, will it be Around Then, anyway? What about a point that comes after both Exactly Then and Around Then? What about Now? What about Ever?

As my mind meanders, twisting and strolling and looking around, as it concocts hypotheticals and just as quickly shoots them down, I also wonder if being a mum is actually in my destiny at all. And then I wonder why I've never felt like I've had permission to say that aloud.

For such a common affliction, affecting up to ten per cent of Australian women, an endometriosis diagnosis can be surprisingly hard to receive. In my case, it came after a bunch of pain rendered me absolutely useless at a similar time every month. (I say similar, because my period was never particularly kind in its consistency.) Every three or five weeks – or every two if it felt like it – my period would come and bring with it a band of cronies who would squash me with pain and fatigue.

It was the fatigue that would arrive first, smacking me on landing. It was never subtle and it never gave much warning. It would come, say hi and make itself at home just like an over-familiar neighbour, thrashing my energy levels until perhaps the fatigue itself fatigued, dissipating until it was time to return again next month. Or next week.

The pain was careless, consistent and powerful in its ability to keep me horizontal for multiple days at a time. It came in waves, like pain often does, both flirty and erratic, never staying long enough for my weeks to be totally invaded, but long enough for each pain-filled punch to land.

I always noted the distinct sense of discomfort that came with my period's arrival. The discomfort was part pain, part sentiment. My body felt heavier; movement took more thought and certainly more energy. I was slow, sluggish and lethargic. For a fleeting moment every month, I didn't recognise myself or my own form.

I was about nineteen by the time I received formal diagnoses of endometriosis and vaginismus within months of each other. The endometriosis diagnosis came post-surgery, as it only can, after it was confirmed that yes, smatterings of endometrial tissue had wedged their way into nooks and crannies beyond my uterus and settled into their cyclical rhythm of painful reminders that they weren't where they should be.

I wonder now if one of the reasons it didn't interrupt my mind or my foray into early adulthood was because I didn't let it. My relationships with endometriosis and vaginismus followed occasionally overlapping paths, each characterised by denial and my firm belief that neither condition could rattle me if I did not want it to. Perhaps it helped, too, that my gynaecologist was undemonstrative in a way I didn't mind, with a no-nonsense decisiveness that I grew to appreciate. She wasn't one to indulge airs and graces; she was matter-of-fact in her delivery of news but thoroughly kind, once I found a way to crack her.

What's funny is that at first, the endometriosis diagnosis gave me no cause for concern, no late-night worry or bubbling angst – until a year after that initial surgery, when I began to understand how its hold on my body could go far beyond fleeting flashes of frenzied pain. That was when I began to understand my fertility was now part of this conversation, but I wasn't.

'And babies?' I asked, with no conviction at all really, as an incidental 'Oh yes!' sort of thing. I had the inflection of someone trying so hard to convey composure, it came out as a kind of squeak.

Considering my words, my gynaecologist kept her eyes fixed to her screen, brushed her hand through the air and told me not to worry. I don't remember her exact reply – it was six years ago now – but I remember the message, and the unintended flippancy with which it was delivered.

We will cross that bridge when we come to it.

With a shrug of the shoulders and a quick smile, she had just given me her prognosis – and all I took from it was an infinite stretch of limbo.

I was twenty at the time, and it had been a year since I had hobbled out of surgery. I found it peculiar that my future – my health – was now being projected in clichés that made little sense. How would I cross that bridge when I came to it when I didn't even know *when* I would be able to do the crossing? What if, by the time I got there, I had missed my window and there was no bridge to cross? Why couldn't anyone just give me a tangible answer to sit with now, so I didn't fixate on nonsensical metaphors about bridges and moats and fertility?

I understood her intention, her sentiment and even her tone. I understood it as much then as I do now, because it's characteristic of every conversation I've had in the years since about my body, fertility and future. The few times I've raised the question around my fertility, be it through an off-hand, self-deprecating comment or a more earnest one wrapped in genuine confusion, it's been met with the same overwhelming response:

This is not your worry to own yet.

A response like that one is infused with good intentions and short-sighted attempts to comfort. After all, no one wants to stoke the stress, inflate the insecurity or encourage the worry when nothing is concrete or confirmed. Why exacerbate concerns about fertility when things could change? When it might not prove to be a problem? When science could catch up or if, when the time comes, you could find another way to parent a child?

Logically, it makes sense. Perhaps, too, it's what I would say if I found myself on the other side of the conversation. But the reality is I'm not on the other side and logic often doesn't help because in cases like these, rationality and emotion are like oil and water, repelling on impact, at odds with the other's essence.

Bridget Hustwaite, the host of *Good Nights* on Triple J and ambassador for Endometriosis Australia, was diagnosed with stage four endometriosis in August 2018, at the age of twenty-seven. When Mich and I interviewed her for *Shameless*, she spoke of the quiet isolation and confusion that comes with trying to have conversations about fertility when you're not yet ready to try to have a baby.

'In my own life and my own experience, I have brought fertility up with every GP and gyno I've visited. And they're always like, "How old are you?" And I tell them I am twenty-eight, and then they ask when I want to have kids. I tell them not now, and they tell me not to worry. That we can worry about it later. But I am worried. I am super worried,' she said.

Considering a world in which young women are encouraged to participate in conversations about fertility is not without headaches. There is always the risk of fearmongering, of our terror being taken advantage of by institutions who see value in our nerves and dollar signs in our uncertainty. But there has to be a happy medium; an arena in which the conversation can prevail, a safe space for women to express concern without fear they will be told to fall pregnant at once or freeze their eggs right away.

Bridget agrees. 'You're either being told "Don't worry about it, you're sweet" or "Get pregnant now, pregnancy helps your symptoms". A lot of women who are diagnosed with endometriosis are told to either get pregnant or have a hysterectomy when they are diagnosed, and those are two complete extremes: two very big, life-changing things. There's no middle ground between those two things, like there's no middle ground in the fertility conversation. But I do want to worry about it, I do want a plan.'

I've always wondered where the other young women are; the ones who harbour the same worries I do but have never been given permission to say them aloud. The ones treading water in a real-life purgatory, where the future feels fickle and the unknown leaves them breathless at night. Where are they and their worries and their confusion? Where did we bury them once they buried their pain? Where are their voices and their hearts and their fear?

I fear the world has gagged them without meaning to, and dismissed their concerns because we didn't know how to navigate a conversation where their anxieties could become their truths.

When I tell someone I'm not sure if I'll be able to have kids, or that I don't know what my fertility looks like now, nor will I in five years' time, I'm not looking for their advice or even their sympathy, because who's to say what's in the illustration of my future? All I want is for someone to tell me my confusion is warranted, my forward-thinking legitimate, that, even though things may work out in exactly the way they are meant to, it's okay to be riddled with worry now. That as a young woman not yet ready to have a child, I am allowed to be vocal about the fear of a day I may be ready, but my body decides I am not.

I want them to agree that for too long, the space between young women and the fertility conversation has been chasmal, that for too long we've been locked out, that for a stupid amount of time people forgot we were a part of it, too. And I want them to share my hope that somewhere in that yawning blank space, we might even be given a place to sit.

Sometimes, in those moments when I look forward, I think about love. I think about the people I love now, the people I will love later and the overlap between them. I think about what my love will be worth, what my currency will be, where my value will lie. Mostly, I think about what will happen if my love is never maternal.

Will there be some binding, inexplicable, all-consuming kind of love I never get to feel? Is there a love that exists that could fundamentally change my identity, that may never flood my veins? Without ever knowing maternal love, will I miss out on something metamorphic? Will my love mean much at all, if it's not cradled around the children I raise?

Of course, my rational brain knows the answer to these things: my love has worth and will always have worth beyond the confines of the maternal. Love is subjective; it is whatever we choose it to be. I know that all love is exposing, that all love is terrifying, that all good love makes you feel vulnerable and naked and defenceless. I know love can be both one big thing and a million tiny moments.

When I look back on the memory of my gynaecologist saying my fertility was a bridge I would come to later, I wonder how the conversation would have transpired if I had rejected that answer entirely. If I had told her I did not want to be robbed of the power to make decisions about my own life, and that my biggest fear was not being betrayed by biology, but instead by a system that did not tell me early enough I needed to have children by a certain age or risk growing old without them.

In the moments I've let myself go there – to envisage a future without a tiny, toothless dictator of my own – I don't feel broken or unhappy or unfulfilled, not yet. I just feel confused, and sometimes a little lonely. I yearn for a place where my angst is validated – for me and for the sisters I do not know, with voices I cannot hear, who have been quietly waiting for their bridge, too.

Fertility will deceive the healthiest bodies and the most positive minds. Fertility might be your bridge-crossing problem or it might give you no problem at all. Your love one day may be maternal, or it may be reserved for others. But no matter the form, no matter the future: that worry you feel now? That worry matters, too.

Being in limbo isn't the end of the story, it is a story in itself – a knotty tale with deep meaning, and perhaps it's time to be vocal about that. To stop feeling muzzled, to tell our doctors and nurses, sisters and friends that we refuse to float in a galaxy of limbo, silence and fear.

I am neither at the start nor at the end of my fertility journey, but what I know now is that my spot within it – in the space between both of those endpoints – is worth something, no matter how young I may be.

MIND AND BODY

A recipe for loneliness

So, you've left high school. The days of sitting in a circle with your girlfriends eating a sandwich someone else made for you are gone. You no longer have any actual commitments at all, really. The school bell's regular intervals have been replaced by a monotonous hum of time, filled with nothing but a diet of McDonald's fries, McMuffins and an existential dread stemming from the suspicion that maybe, just maybe, you're not that special. Actually, you're kind of . . . ordinary. You know this because your university lecturer refers to you and your countless peers by your student numbers only, kind of like farm animals (which, now that you think of it, is a very apt description of the situation).

So, with all that spare time on your hands now, why not whip up this delicious recipe for loneliness? It's bound to impress all those people you won't be entertaining!

Loneliness

Makes: Only one.

Takes: Three years, if you're lucky. Maybe five.

Ingredients:

- 1 whole teenager

- 5000 strangers

- 1 Netflix account (can be shared access if you don't have your own)

- 1 depressingly small (and shrinking) bank account

- A dollop of diminished sense of purpose

- 1 suddenly sluggish metabolism

- A dash of natural, organic change

- 245 heavily edited, faux-aspirational Instagram accounts

- 2 popular television shows that depict what 'friendship in your twenties' apparently looks like

- 2 handfuls of moody quotes, to garnish

Method:

1. Take the teenager and coax them into making important life decisions when their only real priority thus far has been buying boxed wine with a fake ID. Gently nudge them into a three-year university degree where they'll rack up huge student debt and, once condensed, teach them no more than ten days' worth of actually useful information for the workforce.

2. Add in 5000 strangers who all go to the same soulless institution to make the teenager feel as tiny as humanly possible. Simmer in a saucepan on low heat.

3. In a high-powered blender, blitz the following: stupidly late nights watching Netflix (gruesome crime documentaries preferred), the increasingly depressing bank balance and diminished sense of purpose. Set aside to stress about later.

4. Once the teenager is untethered from everything that once made them feel connected to the world, pour in the above mixture. Then, with a teeny-tiny blowtorch, violently scorch their confidence with the flames of a slowing metabolism.

5. When the teenager starts to cry, add a dash of organic change to make them feel like all of their friends are drifting (or better: physically moving!) away. Stir until the teenager's best friend goes on exchange to London, joins a multi-level marketing scheme for essential oils, or decides she's into acid and married men. (Or all three! Mmmmmm, flavoursome!)

6. Remove from heat. Leave to marinate for three to five years, checking in every hour to sign the teenager into Instagram to remind them of how inferior their life is compared with everyone else's. Scroll until the teenager is bombarded with images of high school acquaintances pretending they're not lonely at all over glasses of Aperol Spritz in the sun. Stop when the teenager has fully absorbed the sensation that they're doing this friendship thing totally wrong. For maximum flavour, alternate this with reruns of *Sex and the City* and *Friends* to remind them that a friendship doesn't count unless it comes with a tray of cosmopolitans and daily catch-ups!

7. Garnish as desired with screenshots of Instagram poetry from P. Bodi and Rupi Kaur. Bask in those glorious aromas of loneliness and serve. Enjoy!

MIND AND BODY

A rough and tumble on . . .
influence

On Thu, 23 April 2020 at 11:36 AM,
Zara McDonald <zaramcdonald@shameless.com> wrote:

>>>   Mich. Let's get straight into this one. Talk to me about how you got sucked into a vortex of diet teas at eighteen eeeeek.

On Thu, 23 April 2020 at 11:48 AM,
Michelle Andrews <michelleandrews@shameless.com> wrote:

>>>   I THOUGHT YOU WOULD NEVER ASK!
     Ah, diet teas. I remember them with a foul aftertaste in my mouth and a rather uneasy tummy. I got sucked into that trap *early*. I was struggling with a post-puberty metabolism slowdown (and all the classic body confidence issues that rear their heads at that time) so the concept of a magical tea that promised washboard abs was tantalising. I ordered from the first Australian brand I came across – a true pioneer of hot beverages that made young girls shit themselves – and had to hold my nose as I sipped the stuff down. The packs came with two kinds of teas: a 'colon cleanse' variety (yes . . . really) and another that was something herbal-y that smelled of urine (yes . . . really).
     The weird bit? The disgusting diarrhoea didn't strike me as odd at all.

I was totally swept up in the social media messaging that this was a *detox* and my body was expelling *toxins* and unleashing almighty hell every morning was *glamorous*. Sure, I was cramping every night before bed. Sure, I was feeling exhausted and dehydrated and depleted. But what's a little bit of pain when it comes to attaining that elusive Instagram bod? Pah! No problem at all. Give me another mug, thanks.

I didn't grasp the effect diet teas had on me until a few months later, when I realised I could get the same outcome sans the disgusting taste – all I needed to do was pop five or six Laxette tablets every night before bed. In secret, of course.

Diet teas were my introduction to weight loss pills and journals and charts. They taught me to order stuff online and keep it hidden in your bedside drawer. To sneak around the prying eyes of your parents so they never ask 'What are you drinking, Shell?' To go to extreme, disgusting, painful lengths to lose weight, as if doing so is a game, and one that teenage girls who still get back acne and play *The Sims* should try to win. Diet teas were my gateway drug to eating disorder behaviour. They were so, so easy to buy. And the Australian woman who sold them to girls like me was getting so, so rich.

On Thu, 23 April 2020 at 12:04 PM,
Zara McDonald <zaramcdonald@shameless.com> wrote:

>>>   Isn't it crazy, thinking of how much money is in the game of taking advantage of young women's insecurities?

I can't think of a bigger assault on the minds and bodies of young women in recent years than unregulated influencer activity on Instagram. You know, the influencers who tell their followers that they cured their pre-cancerous cells with food! Or the ones who swear that waist trainers took seven inches off their torso! Or that these gummy bears will grow your hair to double its length in less than seven days!

It's interesting that diet tea was your thorn, because tanning oil was mine. It's interesting, too, that it took me until about the age of twenty-four to even realise it *was* a thorn. I spent so much of my early twenties in the sun, lusting after a tan glorified on Instagram by influencers and brands alike. It was a beauty ideal of the most deathly kind; I was searing my skin, like so many young women do, ignoring the fact that it could kill me because instead I was going to look beautiful!

Maybe we don't lust over diet teas as much as we used to, but something inevitably comes next. We figuratively outlaw one dangerous product or one fucked-up brand, only for another to pop up and take its place. After all, we can push back on diet teas and tanning oil as much as we like, but unless we're getting to the root cause of the issue – you know, the abuse of insecurity – then nothing will ever change. And for as long as I've been on Instagram I've spent my time wondering, *Where are all the adults?*

On Thu, 23 April 2020 at 12:14 PM,
Michelle Andrews <michelleandrews@shameless.com> wrote:

>>> Ah, tanning oil. I found an old bottle with a faded label in the back of my bathroom cabinet the other day. Despite the years that have passed and the ink that has faded, it still screams a promise of 'protect and tan', the biggest oxymoron of them all.

I wonder where the adults are, still. I think Instagram has been regarded with such an eye roll for so long – *look at all these girls taking selfies and wishing they were models* – that people are too busy mocking influencer culture and its subscribers to take note of what's actually happening. If teen magazines were instructing girls to bake their skin in the sun and empty the contents of their bowels into the school toilets, there would be collective outrage. Parents would storm the buildings and demand an editor's head. But influencers on a social media app? Oh, that's just all silly, immature girl stuff. It's all selfies and filters and hashtags, right?

The Space Betw**een**

People underestimated Instagram. They underestimated how much power pretty women could yield on this platform, how many morally bankrupt entrepreneurs were willing to use those women as Trojan horses in order to stuff their pockets with money, and how many girls could be fooled by those Trojan horses.

Sure, people started to get pissed off about diet teas in 2018, but that's only because the victims of Instagram culture – women like Jameela Jamil – were now old enough and wise enough to understand what was happening from the inside out. Before the casualties of the influencer economy found their voices, there was nothing.

And yes, after years of diet teas destroying toilet bowls and young girls' self-esteem, Instagram finally placed bans on them being advertised to girls under the age of eighteen in 2019. But by that point, seven years had already passed since I personally fell victim to the scam. *Seven years.* How many other problematic products have popped up and gained momentum in that time, like peptide-based sun-tanning products that promise a 'safer, darker' tan, when their usage – by design of them encouraging sun exposure and, in some cases, sunbed usage – has actually been linked to an increased risk of melanoma? How many hundreds of thousands of girls are going to buy those before we notice and act?

I'd love to know, because seven years is too fucking long.

What really makes my stomach churn (ha, geddit) is that as soon as you try to tell a brand or influencer that what they're putting out into girls' minds is dangerous, you're labelled a hater and a bully. Just ask Jamil, who has grown all too familiar with the 'dog fight' (her term, not mine) that erupts as soon as you try to hold a powerful social media personality to account.

Why do you think that is? And why do you think normal, everyday women become so defensive of the very Instagram profiles that profit from our self-hatred?

On Thu, 23 April 2020 at 12:33 PM,
Zara McDonald <zaramcdonald@shameless.com> wrote:

>>> Yes! Yes! Everything you just said. And I don't often agree with every single thing you say to me. Lol, kind of kidding, kind of not. People absolutely *did* underestimate Instagram and the women who found power from its feed. They still do.

To your question about why we toss around the word 'bullying' so recklessly when often it's just the pursuit of holding powerful people to account, I think it says a lot about how we don't see Instagram power as a legitimate form of social and cultural power. For example, to build on your comparison between influencers and women's magazines, we see a media company as a faceless, formalised institution with processes and standards. We follow influencers, largely, for their personalities. We see them as everyday people who found power through happenstance, and we are invested in their days, work and relationships. Acknowledging that the people we follow can be problematic and do problematic things can be a hard pill to swallow and some fans feel that criticism personally. That's where the defensiveness comes in, I think. We see ourselves in these people a little bit, thinking of them more as girls next door than women with greater Instagram followings than the biggest news websites in the country.

And so, anyone who holds an influencer to account is deemed a 'bully' or 'woman hater', most often not by the influencer themselves, but by their fans. Someone like Jameela Jamil is accused of being too harsh, too loud, too cutting. We expect her to articulate her passion palatably, mistaking her valid critique of fucked behaviour (hello Kardashians and weight-loss lollipops) as an attack on someone's personality.

On top of that, social media flattens conversations. It removes nuance and detail, and encourages us to talk in absolutes. On Instagram, feminism has been diluted to mean 'women supporting women', when in reality, feminism doesn't mean blindly supporting all women, particularly the ones inflicting harm on young girls. Does that ring true for you? That Instagram and the way it flattens our conversations has a heap to answer for?

On Thu, 23 April 2020 at 12:51 PM,
Michelle Andrews <michelleandrews@shameless.com> wrote:

>>> Oh, god, yes. I mean, I've just looked up the tea brand that sparked LaxativeGate 2012 and not only do they STILL EXIST, their new slogan is 'Boost yourself back to wellness'.

Like, what?! Boost yourself back to wellness . . . with this laxative tea? What aspect of my explosive diarrhoea says 'wellness' to you, exactly?

It only gets worse when you look at everything else the brand is sharing on their feed: pseudo-feminist memes that say 'YES GIRL YES', 'You are braver than you believe, stronger than you seem, smarter than you think' and 'Go with your gut'. Go with my gut where, exactly? To the bathroom because I drank your fucking awful tea? Because that's where my gut is telling me to go right now, you transparent, idiotic charlatans.

I despise how feminism and 'girl power' have been bastardised by Instagram brands in this way. It follows this ridiculously flawed logic that if a woman buys something for herself – not for her partner, friend or child – then that constitutes self-care, and any form of self-care is actually self-love, and self-love is inherently feminist. Forget that she's paying hard-earned money for this shitty product! Or that the product is a cog in the diet machine that tells women that they should above all else be thin! Definitely don't consider the fact that diet culture is a child of the patriarchy! None of that matters! Here, look at our pretty memes!

If you can dream it, you can do it!!!

In an ideal world, young women and girls will do their own research into troublesome products, which will lead them to the right corners of the internet where the opinions of experts with relevant qualifications reign supreme and they won't buy the goddamn diet tea/tanning accelerator/ whatever product becomes a trend next. Only, I know what it's like to be seventeen or eighteen and to lack those necessary critical thinking skills to dig deeper. I also know that it's pretty bloody easy to just accept whatever an influencer is telling you at face value, particularly when you've followed and loved them for years.

I guess the most ironic aspect of this discussion is that by having conversations about influence on a podcast, we ourselves became accidentally, well, influential. How do you feel about our audience size and sway now?

On Thu, 23 April 2020 at 1:06 PM,
Zara McDonald <zaramcdonald@shameless.com> wrote:

>>>   Ha. The elephant in the room, but a good question. I think about our audience size every single day. I think about our reach, and the power we have to do good or bad, and I feel terrified. I'm terrified because I want to do right by the young women who listen to us, and I'm terrified that one day we could let them down.

I've recently been struggling with burnout, as you know. The bigger our podcast has become, the more my mental health has suffered. I love our job, more than I ever thought I could love a job, but the pressure, at times, has felt all-consuming. It's interesting to me when I look back at my own Instagram feed over the last six to twelve months and see the glamour of my own highlights reel. It looks like our trajectory has been easy, quick and glittery. It has been quick, and at times, it is glittery. But it's also been tough. My Instagram account gives no insight into how sometimes the stress has made me physically ill for days on end, or how much I've had to lean into exercise to stay sane, or how much hair I have lost because of worry. I worry about fucking up, I worry about it all falling apart. I worry about all of that happening publicly.

And then, well, I feel guilty. I feel guilty that I don't share enough of the shit times, that I am not using my influence to tell people things aren't always as they seem. But how much of ourselves do we need to hand over and share? How much of ourselves do we owe to people because of that influence? I ask myself those questions all the time.

I do feel like I have gone off on a bit of a tangent, but I guess those are my actual, unfiltered thoughts on our own influence: that I am still reckoning with it.

Now let me ask you: do you think we are 'influencers'? And how intensely do you feel a responsibility to do the right thing when it comes to monetising our work?

On Thu, 23 April 2020 at 1:52 PM,
Michelle Andrews <michelleandrews@shameless.com> wrote:

>>> Oh god I hate this question because I feel like there's no right way to answer it.

Do I think we are influential? Yes. And that terrifies me as much as it does you, but it's also crucial to point to our power and privilege wherever we can, because if we don't, we're effectively dodging the accountability that is ours to carry.

Do I think we are *influencers*? I suppose I hate the word because, in my mind, 'influencer' is synonymous with 'person pushing products they've literally never used before on Instagram'. My siblings use it to describe what we do whenever they feel like riling me up.

I think there's a difference between cultural influencers and consumer influencers, perhaps. As in, there are women and men who are primarily driven by the desire to shape social attitudes (say, artists and poets and athletes) and then there are those who are motivated by the desire to shape spending behaviour (those who consider what images they post on their Instagram grid that day to be their primary form of work). Of course, there will naturally be an overlap between the two kinds of influencer. It's near impossible to be a cultural influencer if you can't support yourself financially, so people like us naturally need to find sponsorship work with brands that they enjoy and trust.

The advertising we do is never the main 'point', though. I would hate for anyone to click out of a one-hour episode and think the only takeaway was whatever we shared in the one-minute ad space. The ads exist to help us put out the podcast every week, so that we can share our analysis of what women are talking about.

I am glad that we devised such clear filters on what brands we will and won't work with from the very beginning, as it means that whenever a pitch pings into our inbox we are instantly on the same page about who reflects our core values, and who just doesn't. I think about the thousands of dollars we've turned down from brands that weren't right for us and I do feel a small sense of pride. We're not here to make women feel worse about their place in the world. Will we always get it right? No, probably not. But it's a conversation we – along with other women we love and admire – are constantly having, and I think if all kinds of influencers prioritised it, then Instagram would be a better place.

We're here to talk to women about the stuff they care about, and if we can recommend a product or brand we like at the same time? Then that's the dream.

Does that distinction between the different kinds of influencers sit well with you? I'll never be one hundred per cent on board with the term, but I feel more comfortable with the idea that perhaps we're not being lumped in with the people who represent everything I dislike about Insta.

On Thu, 23 April 2020 at 2:06 PM,
Zara McDonald <zaramcdonald@shameless.com> wrote:

>>> I think you are right – you've painted an accurate description, but is it bad that I still shudder at the thought of it?

On Thu, 23 April 2020 at 2:31 PM,
Michelle Andrews <michelleandrews@shameless.com> wrote:

>>>   GAH! Okay, same. I try to convince myself that I'm okay with it, but
deep down I'm really, really not lol.

I'm a pretty optimistic person, but when it comes to the future of
Instagram, I do despair. The lucrative sponsorship offers pinging into
most influencers' inboxes are clearly too alluring for them to glance
down at their moral compasses. There will continue to be an onslaught
of venomous advertising that seeks out and targets teenagers, not their
more mature and reasonable older sisters. There will always be shitty
adults who seek to make a quick buck, even if it's at the expense of
impressionable girls.

Wow, sorry, that was depressing.

How do you feel about the future when it comes to the stranglehold
Instagram's influencers and brands have on young women?

On Thu, 23 April 2020 at 2:55 PM,
Zara McDonald <zaramcdonald@shameless.com> wrote:

>>>   This is a really hard one. I would love to end this with some kind of
message about self-love, self-esteem and hope for the future. But
female insecurity will exist as long as the world communicates to young
girls from the tiniest of ages that they aren't skinny enough, toned
enough or *good* enough. And the truth is, vulnerability is really bloody
easy to make money from. So I can't write us a plan for the future,
because in order to do that, I'd be writing a strategy to dismantle the
patriarchy in its entirety.

That said, I think there are things we can do to make the online world
safer for the minds and bodies of young women everywhere. We can
harness the power of public pressure. No influencer is going to change
their habits or what they promote if they don't feel pressured by the

MIND AND BODY

public to do so, or unless it suddenly becomes bad for their brand to align themselves with dangerous products. It works; we've seen it work. We've seen influencers stop promoting things like tanning oils because a collective has spoken loud enough.

Using public pressure, we can fight passionately for this sinister side of Instagram brands, and influencers, to be taken seriously. We can yell loudly about the fact they aren't frivolous entities, but accounts that wield great power and control over a generation of young women. Because when we do that, when we push the actions of these brands and people into the mainstream, we can make the adults sit up and take notice.

We can grab their attention and say, Hey! See what's going on over here? It's messing with the minds of your daughters.

The space between knowing botox is bullshit and wanting it anyway

– MICHELLE –

My umbilicoplasty obsession began at the bottom of my grand-parents' pool.

I was twelve and it was the middle of summer in Frankston, Victoria. I did my very best thinking at the bottom of that pool. It was where life's biggest conundrums – *How do I get Mum to buy me a training bra without actually asking her? Where can I get $7 to buy the latest edition of* Dolly *magazine? How do I open the sealed section without anyone noticing? What's the difference between an organism and an orgasm?* – were solved. I felt calm under that water. The cacophony of cicadas and clangs of lunchtime plates were blanketed into obscurity by all that shiny reflective fluid. It was home to all my lightbulb moments. And this was my most profound: I should get my bellybutton reshaped by a plastic surgeon.

I had known my bellybutton was *a little wrong* for a while. I had only recently seen the photos of Miranda Kerr – petite, flawless, golden Miranda Kerr – walking in the Victoria's Secret runway show alongside other equally petite, flawless, golden women. And in between all the glitter and sequins and pad-tastic push-up bras, it dawned on me: their bellybuttons. *Their dainty, marquise-cut-diamond bellybuttons.* The buttons on those bellies looked nothing like mine.

My bellybutton, for the oh-so-curious, was less marquise-cut diamond and more fleshy mound emerging out of a stomach. I could tell you it was an outie and be done with it, but oh no, reader, my bellybutton was so much more than that. My twelve-year-old bellybutton was a bulbous bauble of a thing – the centrepiece of my tummy, the bane of my pre-pubescent existence.

Now, look. If you were to find photos of my twelve-year-old bellybutton (which you won't, because twelve-year-old Michelle would sooner die than have you catch a glimpse of her exposed tummy, so images of it are as rare as adult women who enjoy Adam Sandler movies) you would lose your eyes in the back of your head. Was it the solar eclipse of bellybuttons? No. It was basically the navel of a heavily pregnant woman on the body of a scrawny, very un-pregnant pre-teen. It really wasn't that bad. I mean, have you ever looked at someone's bellybutton and felt a rush of repulsion? No, you haven't, because you are normal, and I'm confident only normal and respectable humans (with impeccable taste, by the way) will buy this book.

But try telling that to twelve-year-old Michelle.

One measly Victoria's Secret catwalk and I was under the spell. I spent evenings Googling the ins and outs – literally – of my most hated physical feature. I was the human encyclopaedia for bellybutton corrective surgeries, which is a relatively useless area to be an expert in when you're twelve. I pored over every detail I could find – how long umbilicoplasty surgery took, what it cost, the potential risks, what the typical recovery looked like. To hell with a $7 *Dolly* magazine, I needed 4000 American dollars and two morally corrupt parents willing to let their child undergo major plastic surgery in the incredibly noble pursuit of a Miranda Kerr bellybutton.

I had none of those things. All I had were a few gold coins and a tacky Guess purse that remains, to this day, my worst-ever incident of buyer's remorse. Unfortunately, my parents are annoyingly good people with a robust moral fibre that no petulant twelve-year-old can shred, and they insisted my bellybutton was 'cute' and 'not like a cupcake at all'.

I wonder if I was doomed from the beginning, if this life of insecurity was guaranteed from the moment I noticed a body and a face could be 'right' or 'wrong'.

I'm starting to think I was programmed to be this way. That every woman is, really.

I know that if I wanted to be a truly perfect feminist, I would rebel against the ridiculous beauty standards that society foists upon me. I would look at the differences between my partner's 'get ready regimen' (shower; shave face; blast armpits with deodorant; sunscreen face; douse self in fragrance; dress self) with my own (shower; shave legs, armpits, lady region; wash hair; cleanse, exfoliate and moisturise face; moisturise elbows, wrists, knees, ankles; fake-tan body; sunscreen face; apply make-up consisting of primer, foundation, concealer, powder, bronzer, blush, illuminator, setting spray, eyebrow pencil, eyeshadow, mascara, lip balm, lipstick; blow-dry hair; style hair; blast armpits with deodorant; douse self in fragrance; dress self) and feel so appalled that I'd grow my body hair to plait-able lengths in defiance. If I were a perfect feminist – one who cared enough about the hours that have turned into days, that have turned into months, that have turned into years that I've already spent subscribing to an unattainable beauty ideal – I'd feel utterly sick about it. And don't get me wrong, *part of me does feel sick*. But the bigger part of me? The louder, more emotional part? She's shrugging right now. She gets the point, the ludicrousness of it all. She can intellectualise it, write it down, point to the gross chasm that splits how society defines male and female beauty. But she feels fizzy towards the stuff that shackles her to a cosmetic mirror. She's excited to drain her bank account for a new serum, potion or goo that her boyfriend would cackle at the thought of buying. She finds joy in the injustice, actually. It's her *hobby*.

Then there's the next level up, The Serious Beauty Stuff, where brushes and curling tongs are replaced with scalpels and syringes. Warning, reader: this level is where I become quite a terrible feminist indeed; where I relax into the grooves of my true personality, Michelle 'A-Grade-Hypocrite' Andrews.

Let me explain. My partner and I are the same age (actually, I'm one month and thirty days older, a small win for feminism!) and according to the human eye, we have aged at the same rate. We are both on the precipice of ruing the many, many days we forewent SPF as early twentysomethings. Some shit isn't quite sitting where it used to. We are developing little baby wrinkles around our eyes. I'm sure something rather odd is happening to the backs of our hands. And, the real clincher: when we lift our eyebrows in surprise, our foreheads crease into three even grooves. To my knowledge, my significant other has never considered his lines. He has never spoken about them, Googled them or planned an imaginary budget for them. To him, they are invisible. To me, they are a marker of his aliveness – of moments when his hands slapped his knees as he curled over in delight, of moments when his favourite TV show character got killed off, or he was told great news.

Those lines on my partner's face somehow make him more attractive, the bastard. But my three lines? I accidentally catch sight of them in my car's rear-vision mirror and feel angry. I think about fixing them, correcting them, freezing them, filling them. I fret over how they suck up my foundation like a vacuum. I worry what their increasing depth and size might mean for my career. I want them to disappear. I hate them.

Society's number one rule for male beauty is that men only get more attractive – and sexier – as they age. They go from Noah Centineo to Ryan Gosling to Brad Pitt to George Clooney without ever missing a 'World's Hottest' list. More greys? Sexy. More chest hair? Sexy. More pudge around their mid-section? So sexy there's an adorable nickname for it: 'dad bod'.

But for women? Yeah, no. Women are allowed to age in a very particular way: gracefully, *of course*, but with six-weekly hairdresser appointments that cost $200 a pop and botox so carefully administered it makes friends and co-workers wonder, without ever quite knowing for sure. Women *can* be considered beautiful at every age so long as everything stays exactly the same. For women, 'mum bods' are an affliction in need of correction.

I haven't done anything about my three lines. Not yet. For now, they only cost me energy that would be better spent getting my head around what the actual fuck 'franking credits' are. But one day I know they'll cost me money, too, because the older I get, the more I resign myself to the fact that I will get botox. Maybe not until I'm thirty, or even forty, but I know it will happen. That, despite all the very worthwhile arguments against the stuff – *It's poison! Female expression is important! We need to push against the toxic idea that a woman's worth declines with her age!* – I'm not quite strong enough to withstand the pressure.

None of this is ideal. Much to the chagrin of my former rad-fem Gender Studies lecturer, I will never be a trailblazing feminist,

renowned for her brazenness in rejecting bullshit beauty standards. I would apologise to her here and now, but you know what?
The amphitheatre of fucked-up beauty standards is dangerous for
all women, and I, like everyone else, am doing my best. There is
no real protection from the faceless crowd, the rowdy audience,
all that rotten fruit being thrown at us. We've been in the arena
since the day we learned to read, since the day we turned on the
television to see those Victoria's Secret tummies, followed by ads
that instructed us on how to obtain them In Just Six Weeks! And
now? Now there are sharp arrows, and they're coming from all
directions, slicing our fingers as we scroll, as we catch up on our
old schoolfriends' job promotions, break-ups and beach holidays.
They are arrows of laxative lollipops, blowjob lips and dimple-
free thighs, of facetuned Barbie-doll waists.

It's no surprise so many of us are tired, ducking for cover, franti-
cally swapping our credit card details in exchange for armour. So
long as Instagram is the place we share our lives, we can't escape.
Unfollow whoever you like, darling – the algorithms will find
you. They'll remind you of everything you're not.

Like, have you seen your teeth lately? They're a little yellow from
all that black coffee those wellness influencers told you to drink.
You can buy an at-home teeth-whitening kit, you know. Sure, it's
flogged exclusively by people who have pristinely white veneers
and therefore cannot and do not use at-home teeth-whitening
kits, but don't get bogged down in the details, silly! And while we
have you . . . wanna buy a booty band? Just make sure you don't
grow that peach too much, hun, 'cos nobody wants cellulite. Oh
no, you have cellulite already?! Don't worry, we've got a totally
unregulated cream that will melt those pockets of fat (and maybe
your skin) right away. Speaking of skin, you're looking a little pale,
babe! Here's a tanning oil to get golden brown. Only, now we call
it a 'sunscreen oil' because everybody knows sun tanning is linked

to melanoma and our PR team says that's 'bad for brand'. *Boring.* Anyway, this is the exact same product with a shiny new label because we want to make money. Now that we're on the topic of money, how much have you got? Those lips could do with a bit of collagen, don't you think? If needles aren't your thing, we've got a plastic surgeon who calls himself 'The King of Tits' and he wants to redo your breasts, too. They'll post little sad face emojis over your nipples in the 'before' shot, and stars over your nipples in the 'after' shot!

Instagram tricked an entire generation of women. We signed up under the promise of connection, but what we got was a portal of chicanery; an alternate reality filled with avatars of people like us, only better. A world where everything seemed a little brighter, a little more beautiful, with no explanation of how. We thought we were stepping onto a bridge made of pixels and filters with a pot of belonging at the end, but really, that bridge led to a swamp; a place that slowed us down with the sludge of everything we're not, everything we're told to aspire to be.

We're on a monotonous wheel of make-believe, overflowing with women who are busily peddling bullshit hair-vitamin gummies despite the $2000 extensions sewn into their scalps.

As ridiculous as I know it is, if I can afford to do it, I will one day invite a needle into my face. I will wince through the pain. I will deplete my savings account. At the same time, I will be insulating my career in the public eye from an early capitulation, because I know that women's wrinkles and the mainstream media have the compatibility of a mouse and a tiger. The gravity and sadness of that sentence is not lost on me. Effectively, I will be paying the price to subscribe to a game no woman can ever win. But you know what?

I will keep moving, because life is littered with contradictions, and this one might never fully make sense to even me.

I will also, I suspect, feel like a failure to other women.

It seems particularly cruel that, after all their efforts to dodge the arrows, women are judged the second they give in to the pressure that encircles them, as if they are letting the sisterhood down when they wave their hands in the air and ask for a little respite. I don't want to feel shitty about myself for considering cosmetic procedures or plastic surgery. Right now, what I really fucking want is to buy a sturdy metal helmet. (I'd also quite like $1000 to be magically deposited into my bank account every twelve or so months, because succumbing to botox is, you know, rather expensive.)

So, what can we do for each other? Well, the women who decide botox isn't for them can stop the sneering and the whispering when they hear someone has had work done. They can be a little more understanding and empathetic towards their fellow comrades, who are ultimately human. They can approach these things with compassion, because what one woman decides to do with her face and body reflects a lifetime of pressure. And we can't ever truly know what that pressure has looked like for another woman – we know just a sliver of each other's long and complicated stories. All we can do is trust that whatever decision another woman makes is the right one for her.

As for the women like me, the ones who have already strapped on this armour or who know they will one day? We can also take responsibility for the pressure we feel. We can choose to swallow it, instead of magnifying it. We can stop sending the arrows in other women's directions. We can be mindful of how we speak to our daughters and nieces. We can stand up from our seats and walk out the amphitheatre door. We can be honest about what we've had done so that our friends are never tricked into thinking we won a genetic lottery that they never had the chance to enter. We can avoid advertising the outright lie that one syringe full of paralysing chemicals is going to undo decades of body image issues. We can acknowledge that in some cases, it might even compound the noxious thoughts.

We can talk to each other. We can make it our mission to give each other compliments on things that have nothing to do with how we look. We can watch each other's backs, knowing that most of us never asked to be here.

We can all be a little gentler on each other.

If we don't, how will we ever make it home?

Is he a closet sexist?
A checklist

Want to figure out if that man is just a teeny-tiny bit sexist? Let's play a game! Tick the boxes for the phrases you've heard leave his mouth.

- ☐ 'Women are funny, I've just never found a female comedian I've enjoyed watching.'

- ☐ 'I just don't understand why we need a statue of a female footy player.'

- ☐ 'I don't have a problem with women playing footy, I just don't like watching it because I don't think it's very good.'

- ☐ 'I'm just not sure if female commentators need to be commentating the men's game. Why don't they just put the women on the women's games?'

- ☐ 'I don't like the sound of her voice.'

- ☐ 'I could easily take a few points off Serena Williams.'

- ☐ 'She screeches a bit too much.'

- ☐ 'The old ball and chain.'

☐ 'It feels like this "#MeToo" stuff has gone a bit too far, if you ask me.'

☐ 'I hate to say it, but sometimes I think men can't do much anymore. My mates say they're scared to talk to women in public now.'

☐ 'She's a ball breaker.'

☐ 'I'm not saying I agree with all of them, but some men's rights activists make good points.'

☐ 'Sometimes I think things were better the way they used to be.'

☐ 'It's a joke. I don't know why she can't see it's a joke.'

☐ 'She seems to have a lot of opinions.'

☐ 'I have to babysit the kids this weekend. The misso is away.'

☐ 'Why are you wearing so much make-up?'

☐ 'She's gagging for it.'

☐ 'Well how was she so stupid to get pregnant in the first place?'

☐ 'The company has never had a female director? Well, what if all those men were just the ones who were better for the job?'

☐ 'I'm not sure the gender pay gap really exists. I mean, if women choose to work hard and play the game then they can earn just as much as men.'

☐ 'I'm all for raising women up, but not at the expense of men.'

- [ ] 'You might say women are too emotionally charged for some positions.'
- [ ] 'I can't put my finger on it, but she just seems difficult.'
- [ ] 'We had Julia Gillard as a prime minister. Wouldn't you say that means we don't have a gender problem?'
- [ ] 'I've heard she's the town bike.'
- [ ] 'Who wears the pants?'
- [ ] 'Of course I care about women! I have a daughter!'
- [ ] 'What about International Men's Day?'
- [ ] 'Like, obviously no means no, but there's a bit of a grey area sometimes don't you think?'

So! How does he stack up?

1–4 boxes: Nah, probably not a sexist. Just a bit shit sometimes.

5–10 boxes: It's not looking good. Probably needs to read up on some Gloria Steinem.

11–20 boxes: Fuuuuuuuuuuuck.

21–29 boxes: Run! Run as fast as you can! Before he can tell you that you run like a girl.

VOICE

The space between finding your voice and feeling self-conscious about having one

− ZARA −

About a year ago, a friend sent me a text. He had been at drinks the previous evening and, well, he'd found it a little awkward. Some of the people there were talking about me, and they didn't have streams of kind things to say. They were laughing about my work. They poked fun at the podcast, the publicness of what we do and the way, just weeks earlier, I had struggled to contain my falling tears when talking about my long history of hating sex.

I don't know why he told me. I don't know why his friends were unkind. I don't know why they cared about my job or my words or my experiences enough to spend their Friday evening pulling me apart. I do know, though, that it wounded me in a way I wasn't ready for. I felt like someone had winded me, like I'd been punched and kicked and stomped on. But instead of feeling the physical blows of each pummel, I felt the rising ache of humiliation. Was I just an idiot? Was the sum total of their opinions worth more than the belief I had in myself?

It was a Saturday evening, and I was due out an hour later to have drinks with my friends. I didn't make it out of the house. I called my mum, and then I called my sister. What was I doing? I asked them. Was I stupid and loud and obnoxious? Was I lame and embarrassing and worth nothing at all? Was I a stain on the very industry I loved so much?

They held me close with their words. If the thought of distant acquaintances sitting around a kitchen table belittling me made me feel small, weightless and worthless, then my mother and my sister worked meticulously to piece back together the shards of my confidence. They breathed life into my self-esteem with every assurance that my voice was worth something. That it isn't unattractive to stick your neck out, that opinions are important, that finding and keeping an edge to my voice makes me, well, me.

It was strange that, in a period of my life where my voice was both my job and my currency, I still needed the people around me to remind me of the importance of speaking up and feeling confident in the things I have to say. Stranger, perhaps, because the most common question Michelle and I now receive is all about this.

'How do you find your voice?' women ask us over email or via Instagram DMs or in person. 'How do you get to a point where you feel confident in the things you have to say and the way you want to say them?'

Sometimes I say it's time or reading, other times I will mention having conversations with the people I love about issues I don't. Rarely do I add the following: it's one thing to look for your voice, but it's another thing entirely to find parts of one but still feel self-conscious enough to stifle its volume and reach.

Even though every Monday I sit in front of a microphone and use my voice as my job, I often don't feel clever or confident or considered. I scarcely admit this but I spend significant amounts of time questioning the things I have to say and the way I want to say them. I am chronically unsure of myself and I have trouble shaking the lingering embarrassment that comes from airing my opinions and putting myself into the spotlight. My job makes me feel vulnerable and exposed.

When I cast my mind back to that Saturday evening, it's little wonder I took such deep, inherent offence to the things that were said about me. After all, those insult-hurling acquaintances had successfully hit my biggest insecurity: why would anyone listen to anything I had to say, anyway?

My early twenties have been characterised by often being the loudest female in the room and feeling self-conscious about being the loudest female in the room.

Growing up, my parents had a remarkable ability to teach me to say whatever I wanted to say. Sure, their great priority was that my siblings and I stayed kind and humble, but second to that was their subtle, quiet encouragement for us to think for ourselves and find a way to articulate those thoughts aloud.

They created a safe space where we felt comfortable questioning the religious beliefs we were raised on, where we could corner them into divulging who they vote for and why, and for my sister and I to find feminism in a way that meant every dinnertime conversation somehow became almost irrationally political. By virtue of the space they built around me, I found a voice that was loud, passionate, stubborn and just a tiny bit obnoxious. In the world they built for me, I thought I had found the only voice I would ever need. It was the other world, the one that existed outside the walls of our home, that would later tell me my voice would need a bit of tweaking.

By the time I was a teenager, the world had started telling the young women around me that being a woman with opinions – and loud ones at that – was certainly the most unattractive kind of human you could be. When I was nineteen, people jokingly started to refer to me as 'Mrs Opinions' by virtue of the fact I held – you guessed it – views about the world. When Michelle was twenty and started her wildly popular blog, *The 20s Diary*, she purposefully kept it a secret for months because so many of her male friends at the time said she was 'mouthy'. When my sister tried to contribute ideas in a job she held at university, they used to dismiss her ideas because she was usually 'too emotional'. One of my girlfriends, Brittney, acquired the nickname 'Brittney-Brattney-Brains-Haines' because she was outspoken when she was a kid. Shameless Media's producer Annabelle Lee recalls being told she wasn't allowed to have opinions about problematic sportsmen because she didn't play sport. Another girlfriend, Sophie, remembers a select few male teachers at high school eye-rolling at her propensity to raise her hand and ask questions in class. My younger cousin Emily found herself sucking up to whoever branded her 'bossy' at school for fear of being disliked.

The message the world was sending to all of us was clear, if not a little deafening: women are better when they are smaller and less unruly, when they are quiet and meek and pure, when they don't veer outside the lines of the obliging woman.

As I got older and looked towards carving a career in the media, I looked at the women who were front-facing, with voices I respected and careers I was desperate to emulate. Women who were clever and charismatic, who were passionate and articulate and professional. I looked at them and wondered how I could possibly do the job they do while handling the subtle but brutal sexism that came their way. How could I possibly make my voice heard without inviting the world to tell me to shrink?

I would look at high-profile AFL writer Caroline Wilson, a Walkley Award–winning Australian sports journalist, who couldn't dodge the thrashings of sexism that came from being a woman with a personality in the public eye. I would consider what happened to her in 2008, when fellow football media personality Sam Newman attempted to mock her by putting a photo of her face on a lingerie-wearing mannequin in a segment for *The* [AFL] *Footy Show*. I would consider her words a whole decade later, when she delivered the Andrew Olle Media Lecture, and said she was forced to stifle her own fury.

'I was criticised for taking that episode so personally and speaking up about it to colleagues and bosses at Channel 9,' she said. 'My own newspaper said nothing to me about it for a week.'

A high-profile woman with a high-profile voice, being told to shrink.

I looked, too, to another sports journalist, Erin Molan, who in 2014 was asked live on *The Kyle & Jackie O Show* how many sportsmen she has had sex with. In the same segment, a caller was put through who asked Molan whether she'd had a boob job. Affronted, Molan noted it was 'a weird opening question' before asking whether the caller had listened to what she said about football on *The* [NRL] *Footy Show*.

'No one is listening,' co-host Kyle Sandilands replied.

I considered how when, some five years later, a rumoured rift between Molan and fellow commentator Andrew Johns was leaked to the media, the *Daily Mail* led with a headline that read: 'Erin Molan's "giggling and constant talking over other footy commentators" is why league immortal Andrew Johns "can't stand" working with her – and he refused attempts by Nine bosses to cover up the rift.'

Another high-profile woman with a high-profile voice, being asked to shrink.

I looked to journalist Lucy Zelić who, during the soccer World Cup, fended off rape and death threats after she was accused of 'over-pronouncing' players' names.

I cast my eye to politics, where former prime minister Julia Gillard was called a 'witch', and was the subject of a Liberal National Party fundraiser menu that served up quail with 'small breasts, huge thighs and a big red box'. I looked to the 2016 presidential election, and considered the *New Republic* running a story titled, 'Why Do So Many People Hate the Sound of Hillary Clinton's Voice?'

High-profile women, high-profile voices, all asked to shrink.

You'll notice these women are all white, too. Because when I looked to the women who didn't look like me – women who experience not just misogyny but racism, too – most weren't even afforded the privilege of a platform. And the ones we did give space to? Well, we didn't just ask them to shrink, we squashed them completely. Women like Yassmin Abdel-Magied, a Sudanese-Australian writer, former engineer and structural change activist, who was driven out of her own country because of a tweet that drew fair attention to our horrendous treatment of asylum seekers.

I considered them all carefully as I sought to build and craft my own voice, as I became more sure of who I was and the things I wanted to say. I considered them all carefully, and wondered: if the world preferred these impressive and experienced women to be quieter and more obliging, what hope does any woman have against a structure that tells us we are worth more if we sit down and shut up?

On that Saturday evening when I learned people were mocking the publicness of my voice, I also called Michelle. I didn't have the backbone she had, I told her. I didn't know how to do this job without caring, deeply, about what people thought of me. She coached me through it in the delicate way she always does, calmed my breathing, and then told me to call my boyfriend.

'Oli will want to know about this,' she said.

I went quiet for a little bit. Oli, at this point in my life, had been my boyfriend for seven weeks. For five of those, he had been overseas. I loved him, and had told him as much. Our relationship was new but it was strong. There were few things I hadn't already told him, few topics I felt too embarrassed or awkward to raise.

Until . . . well, until then.

Oli was out with his friends, I told her. I couldn't interrupt him.

What I really meant was this: Oli was out with his friends, and we hadn't yet reached that pivotal point in any relationship that is calling the other in a moment of complete vulnerability. We hadn't yet needed to lean, with full force, on each other, to bury ourselves deeply in the other. It felt too early to tell him that some things could shake me, that I wasn't the tenacious independent woman I had been pretending I was.

While I'd spent my early twenties crafting my political voice, I realised I had neglected to shape the more personal voice that articulated to people that sometimes I needed them, and sometimes I needed them desperately. At Michelle's insistence, I messaged Oli anyway. He came quickly, and smothered me with the kind of love that flooded me with relief.

In my teenage years, I thought I was a good friend. I could laugh when my friends laughed, cry with them when their tears came, and be in their corner when they needed me to cower with them. I had their back. My mistake, I realised as I reached my twenties, was that I never allowed them to have mine. Growing up, I clung to this deeply misguided idea that withholding your deepest fears, worries and sources of stress from those around you was the kindest thing you could do. I was the private friend, a brick wall masquerading as a teenager. I didn't need their help because I didn't want to be their burden.

At twenty-one, when the tightly woven fabric of my life began to fray, I realised what confused logic that was. Prompted by family illness, my own health problems and heartbreak, I made the choice to let people in. Telling my friends I felt vulnerable deepened those relationships in a way I had not anticipated.

It may then sound surprising that I did not apply this logic or experience to my romantic relationships at the start of my twenties. For much of my early years in a relationship, I was dogged in protecting my pride, in keeping the walls insulating my vulnerability high and close.

When Gillian Flynn published her third novel, *Gone Girl*, in 2012, she introduced the zeitgeist to the concept of the Cool Girl: the girl we all idolise, but who exists solely for the benefit of the male gaze. In the Cool Girl, Flynn articulated everything I despised about dating culture. The Cool Girl was hot and funny and easygoing, she liked sex and partying and hotdogs. The Cool Girl liked sport and never got jealous. The Cool Girl never had overly political opinions, was understanding and independent and, above all, emotionless. Young men craved the Cool Girl.

At eighteen, I found Flynn's parodic concept of the Cool Girl revolutionary in a world that celebrates the woman who never speaks out of turn, who is both easygoing and self-sufficient. Here was I, a woman who was rarely funny and not always easygoing, who largely found (and still finds) sport boring and parties exhausting, indirectly given permission to *be*. To exist outside the lines of the Perfect Woman, to be unruly and flawed and opinionated and ordinary. I promised myself to never pretend to be otherwise in order to chase the affection of a man. What I was doing, though, by pretending I didn't have needs in my romantic relationships, was playing into the Cool Girl narrative by purporting to not need anyone.

In the hours after finding out my mum was sick, I remember wanting my then-boyfriend to come over but didn't bother asking because he was with his friends that evening, and I was terrified of being the young girlfriend who pulled him away. I remember, too, being nervous to ask for his company after having surgery for the first time for endometriosis, because he was with a new, different group of friends, and what if they thought I was too attached to him?

I remember wanting him both of these times, not so much because of pain or fear or desire for company, but because I was desperate to be chosen. I wanted to be loved in the most obvious, literal, affirming way. I had needs and vulnerabilities, but I also wanted to be self-contained. With all of those forces working against each other, how could I admit I needed to be cared for? That in actual fact, I craved it? My natural, human desire to depend on someone else for love filled me with shame and guilt, as if it were anti-feminist, as if it made me needy and dangerously co-dependent.

But I was wrong. My feminist pendulum had swung too far. I wasn't trying to be independent for my own sanity and pride, but I was, as journalist Lucia Osborne-Crowley wrote for *Meanjin* in 2019, practising a form of 'non-dependence'. I wasn't trying to be independent because I wanted to be strong, I was being non-dependent for fear of being labelled too needy, too emotional, too demanding, too female, too *much.*

'I use the phrase "non-dependence" here because I need to make desperately clear that we are not talking about independence, not really,' Osborne-Crowley wrote. '"Independence" is the wrong word for this evasive quality we are taught to chase. It is not independence at all because true independence is inward-looking and self-defining. What is being asked of us here is wholly dreamt up by others. Performing non-dependence is not about us at all, but rather about reading him carefully enough to know exactly what kind of un-needy-ness he – ironically – needs.'

On the Saturday evening that Michelle bellowed down the phone and told me I needed to let Oli in, that he needed to know when I felt rattled and exposed and sad and scared, I took her advice, went against my own troubled instincts and let the walls caging my vulnerability collapse around me. In that moment, I realised that having needs does not make you inherently needy, and that being dependent on another is part of the human experience: it's central to connection. But here's the other thing we tell women about their voices: that if they have basic human needs, and if those needs are emotional and we say them aloud, then we are a burden, a strain, too heavy a load. That we are taking up too much space in the world.

What's obvious to me now, and perhaps what has been obvious to you throughout this entire piece, is that sometimes it can be hard not to absorb the very messages you're trying to push back on as a vocal feminist. The patriarchy's veneration of 'likeable' women skews our perspectives, warps our sense of self and widens the chasm between who we think we should be and who we want to be. I internalised two ideas that are holding the patriarchy in place today: that it is unattractive to be the one who speaks the loudest, and that if you are a woman with basic human and emotional needs, expressing them makes you needy by default. But of course, I know both of those things are flatly untrue.

I learned two pretty brutal lessons on the evening someone else's opinion of me threatened to overwhelm my self-esteem. The first was the importance of listening to close friends and family when the manifestation of those external voices started thundering in my ear, drowning out any sense of rationality or logic. And the second? Well, I spent so much time internalising this idea that if I had a shameless and decisive voice then I could not and would not be liked that I ignored the fact that if I liked myself enough, the opinions of others would suddenly carry very little weight.

It would be foolish – and, to be frank, wholly arrogant – to think now, at the age of twenty-six, my voice has a fixed form of any kind. My voice is in flux, being built with time, experience and perspective. Don't get me wrong, I don't yet feel completely at ease but I feel *better*. Even as we have a cacophony of voices in our ears telling us as women to sit down and be quiet, there are few things more powerful than using our own voices loudly, thoughtfully and unapologetically.

Gillian Flynn used her voice to push back on how we glorify the likeable woman, manufacturing the Cool Girl trope as a comment on what men want women to be. Erin Molan is still a fixture of radio and television in Australia, and her voice and her smarts and her passion for sport are broadcast to millions of people each week. Julia Gillard now has a podcast. Caroline Wilson does, too. And as for Yassmin Abdel-Magied, who had more stacked against her than any white woman in this conversation? She now boasts a by-line in some of the world's biggest and best news publications and never stopped tweeting. Sure, they were told to sit down and shut up, but none of them actually sat down and not one of them decided to shut up.

Because when we like ourselves and, subsequently, all the things we have to say? That outside commentary becomes white noise, meaningless clutter, specks of floating dust on an otherwise clear day.

A letter to my future daughter

– MICHELLE –

From the moment you can speak, I want you to tell the world what you want.

Always with your manners, always with kindness, but always with honesty, too. I want you to ask for things. To question things. To poke and prod the corners of your mind, and to speak loudly whenever the space you push into unfurls a sea of curiosity.

I also want you to tell the world what you *don't* want. Master the word 'no' (unless we're discussing those peas on your plate). 'No' is a tiny word, isn't it? You can spell much bigger words than that already, but this word is a special one that I want you to practise. Use it when your gut screams out that something's wrong. Say it again and again if you need to. Your mum is old and still struggles with that little word sometimes. I think you can show me how to be better.

Let's talk about climate change over dinner with your father (but don't chew with your mouth open, please). Tell us precisely what you think. I want you to challenge us. Why do some big people in power care more about money than humans? Why aren't we more upset and angry about the people held in Australian camps – prisons – for desperately fleeing poverty and violence in their home countries? Why do little girls' T-shirts tell them to be pretty princesses, when little boys are told to dream big? Why did Ms Mason at kindy tell you to stop being bossy, when she's never said that to Matthew or Noah? Why do all the people in the government look the same? Why do all the really rich people look the same? Why do all the people on television look the same? And why do so many of them get angry when you point that fact out?

I want you to get grumpy with me when I say something stupid. And I will, I'm afraid, say something outdated and foolish at some stage. I'm sorry about that. The brilliant thing about you – and your friends – is that you have so much to teach your dad and me, and all of the other adults. You burst onto the scene with your great, big, enormous hearts and we need you to use those grubby little fingers to point to the spaces where ours have gone chilly. You will be the antidote to our adult cynicism, an injection of simplicity into all of that grown-up mumbo jumbo. I promise that when you challenge me, I will try to open my eyes and see things through yours. Hold on to the empathy and compassion that is pumping through your veins. That stuff is golden magic. It is your superpower. It is rare. We need more of it in this world.

Now, here's the tricky part, where I want you to pay close attention to your mum. Here, give me that iPad for a sec. When you do speak up with that glorious voice of yours, I want you to think about the grey areas. Can you see them? They're hard to spot, sometimes. That's okay, because the main thing is that we keep seeking out the bits of grey. Even when it's tiring, or scary, we need to go looking for them, okay? People on the internet don't like the grey space too much, especially on that social media app you hear your mum whisper ugly, adult words about (please don't tell Grandma). You know the one – the one with the blue bird. There isn't much grey to be found there. Just a lot of people parroting their deep, dangerous reds in

280 characters or fewer. Look out for these people, sweetheart, and be wary of them. Remember all that magic in your veins. Don't let their words dry the golden stuff up.

I promise to go looking with you, and that Dad will come with us, too. The only time we don't look for the grey is when Mum or Dad's teams are playing in the footy, okay? That's the exception. The only one, I promise. Otherwise, let's go!

Before we leave, make sure you pack your ears. Yes, you goose, the ones on your head. Don't leave them at home. Those ears are important; they are like metal detectors for the grey areas. You need to use them if you want to understand other people better, especially the people who don't look like you. Everybody in this world has something to offer, something to teach us, and if you don't use your ears, how will you ever hear what they have to say? Listen very, very carefully to the people who are hurt, the people who are angry. And when what they say makes you feel defensive, don't you dare turn away. It's easy to turn our backs on the people who are telling us to be better. Only cowards turn their backs, though. Brave girls listen even more carefully than before. And you're brave, aren't you?

I think you are.

It will take lots of courage to speak up unwaveringly and unapologetically in this world. People will try to make you feel silly doing so, but they are fearful of you, my girl. You are the lion, and they are the sheep. They know you are clever and bright, and will try to dim your glow and silence your voice. Don't let them. You will need to display little moments of conviction in the face of discomfort, again and again, sometimes in front of people who will belittle you and doubt you, but I know you can do it.

Don't ever let anyone tell you that your opinion doesn't matter. Because it does. Your voice belongs here. I want you to use it. In your relationships, with your boss, with yourself.

You have a lot to say. So say it boldly.

29 ways you might be an imperfect feminist in your twenties

1. You apologise for not having make-up on, as if your face *au naturel* is offensive.

2. You buy (or borrow) at least one feminist book a year, but does it ever get prioritised over that sugary 'chick lit' book about a woman having sex with her husband's brother? Ahhhh, nah.

3. You still use the term 'chick lit' to describe books written by female authors.

4. If you're single and straight, you'll probably put 'must be taller than me' as the number one priority for a male partner. This makes very little sense, and reinforces the idea that women should be smaller than the dudes they date, but to hell with intellectualising this – you'll be dead before you date a man shorter than you. DEAD.

5. You go on dates and bank on the man paying for you. If he doesn't offer, you'll be a little offended for the rest of the week.

6. Despite being on Bumble, you do not like messaging first. Why? Because it's the *man's job* to text first. If you think about how ridiculous that is for too long you'll give yourself a headache.

7. A husband (or wife!) is no financial plan, but you can't help thinking it would be . . . nice.

8. You still shave. Like, everywhere. You know that female body hair is no more unhygienic than male body hair but, well, you do it anyway.

9. You get a smug kick out of men thinking they actually need to open doors for you or wait for you to enter the office lift first.

10. You're probably not that great at changing tyres. You've been taught to do it. You should know. You just, somehow . . . don't.

11. You've dreamt about what your wedding will look like far more often than what your actual married life will.

12. You read the *Daily Mail* sidebar of shame on the way to work and *perversely enjoy* scrolling through the paparazzi photos of women 'flaunting' their 'pert derrières'.

13. You fake orgasms because your desire to people-please outweighs the greater good.

14. Sometimes you catch yourself accidentally slut-shaming reality TV contestants.

15. And while we are on that, you spend too much time watching *The Bachelor*.

16. You've once found yourself in a debate passionately arguing that the Kardashians are 'empowering'.

17. You have spent more than ten minutes editing an Instagram photo before.

18. You will almost definitely have a situationship with a closet misogynist and giggle awkwardly when he says female athletes 'aren't that good to watch anyway'.

19. Sorry, but if you're like us, you probably hate reverse parallel-parking, too.

20. Sometimes you'll joke that you do, in fact, hate all men.

21. You don't ask for what you think you're worth, because you're worried about looking like a young, female greedy-guts.

22. You have, once before, blamed your very valid anger and emotion on having your period.

23. You have also, once before, referred to your period as 'blow-job week'.

24. You spend more time being little spoon than big spoon.

25. If you see a spider you patiently wait for the closest man to sort it the fuck out.

26. You've already decided your children will take your partner's surname because it'll save you a loooooot of hassle in the long run.

27. You're semi/kinda/maybe relying on someone else to figure out the whole 'investing money' thing for you.

28. You sing along to Eminem songs, even when the lyrics are actually kind of depraved.

29. Your feminism has, sometimes, been reserved for only those who look like you. And although you read this dot point with pangs of guilt, the better part of you knows that whatever you're feeling right now doesn't even scratch the surface of what Black, Indigenous, disabled and trans women experience every day. You know within your heart that if you truly want to become a better feminist you will need to stand up for all women. You also know you need to do the work to get there, and that that work is never truly done.

The space between alcohol, my friends and me

— ZARA —

'Hey, so I think I'm going to go home,' I say into the ear of a friend who is dancing clumsily by the bar at which we have spent the last few hours frequenting.

'You're WHAT?' she yells in return, pretending she can't make out my words, when in reality I suspect her intention is to draw attention to my exit.

'Ha, yeah. I think I'm going to go,' I say, a little more sheepishly this time.

'NAH! Don't go. Guys, tell her not to go,' she shouts not in my direction, but in the direction of the others we arrived with.

I'm leaving again.

A crowd of four people begin to circle, looking at me about as intently as tipsy people can, urging me to stay.

'Already?!'

'But you're not even working tomorrow!'

'I'll buy you another drink.'

'Stay, it'll be fun!'

Their words mash together in a messy but unified plea. *Of course you should stay. Where else could you possibly need to be?*

They're right. I don't have work tomorrow, I imagine they will have fun far into the early hours of the morning and it is, in the grand scheme of nights out, an early hour to leave. Also: I want to be the person who wants to stay. I want to be the person who joins them at a gross hour in a desolate corner of McDonald's, already reminiscing on the silly things that happened in the hours between our first and last drinks. I would love to sit next to them in those sticky, stale booths and giggle about how one of us tripped on the dance floor, or another spent $150 on Fireball shots, or one more mouthed off when a stranger got a little too close for comfort.

But I'm tired. Physically, yes, but mentally, too. I'm tired and *I'm leaving again*. I'm no stranger to their late-night pitch to stay out, in the same way I imagine they are no stranger to my early-evening plea to go home.

We are standing in the middle of an overcrowded, chaotic dance floor and I wonder why I don't just tell them how I'm feeling. I think about it for a moment, and ponder what I would say. Would I tell them that at some point in the last six to twelve months I stopped wanting to spend my Saturday nights drinking and losing track of time as it cycles into the early hours of the morning? Would I explain that alcohol feels more alienating than inviting now I'm in my mid-twenties? That I feel diminished by it rather than inflated by it? That it makes me feel anxious, or that when I am drinking I never feel like I'm being outrageous enough or fun enough or funny enough?

I consider having that conversation and then remember why I don't tell them: because we're in our twenties, and our relationships with alcohol are defined by denial. We don't talk about how or why we consume it, or about why our friendships are often

dependent on it. We don't consider the hold it has over our interactions or our confidence, our weeknights or our weekends. Each
new drink is a gateway to socialising, a signifier of being young,
carefree and free from inhibition. Basically, drinking is fun, so
stop overthinking it, yeah?

And so I half-heartedly agree to 'just one more' drink in the
effort to prove I'm not boring or uptight or too serious for a good
time, as if one more vodka soda can undo an entire mid-twenties
identity crisis. I sip on my drink quickly, dance with as much
enthusiasm as I can muster given I don't actually want to be there
and call it for the second time. This time, no one circles and no
one begs me to stay, because this time, they know it's not worth
their energy.

I bid my goodbyes – a kiss here, a hug there, a promise to be
in touch in the morning – and snake my way out of the bar. I'm
on the footpath now, my eyes scanning traffic for the Uber driver
who says he has arrived. As I walk towards him, I find myself
consumed by a familiar concoction of relief and guilt.

I'm leaving again.

I don't want to be inside the bar, but I do want to *want* to be
inside the bar. It's a strange sense of failure, really: my mid-
twenties aren't as wild, carefree or defined by as many silly,
drunken nights out as I thought they would be as a teenager.

Yes, I think to myself as I sink into a stranger's back seat, it feels
like failure. I can't shake the feeling my social life isn't worth
anything if it doesn't look like what it used to. As if I am stuck in
social Siberia. And if I'm no longer fulfilled socially in the way all
my friends seem to be, what does that mean for our interactions?
For our future? For the basis of our friendships?

I rest my head against the back seat and caution myself against
spiralling too far. *You are allowed to leave in the same way they are
allowed to stay.*

The guilt, I know, will linger into the morning, far beyond the moment I jump into bed and let myself slip into sleep. I know this because I have been here many times before. I know, too, that I will wake in the morning and go through the motions once again, texting them to touch base about the rest of their night.

How did it end up? What time did you get home? They have sore heads and droopy eyes, they tell me, and wasn't I smart to go home when I did? They express small shards of self-loathing, knowing they are about to waste one of their only days off lying in bed feeling battered. I know this, because up until a year ago, the sore-headed person receiving that message was me.

'Is this what your mid-twenties are for?' they will ask themselves, buried deep in their doona on a Sunday afternoon, wondering if they are wasting their time, energy and years on drunken evenings out. The nausea will settle into their veins, and the guilt will settle into mine, and we'll all stare into mugs of coffee, convinced we're doing something wrong, certain that the other is doing it right. If only one of us would speak up, and say what we were actually thinking.

In defence of ghosting out of a friend's party

Dear friend,

I write this to you from my Uber ride home. It's 12.30 am and my feet hurt. I'm also concerned one of your half-cooked cocktail sausages has given me salmonella. Can you get salmonella from a cocktail sausage? What's even *in* a cocktail sausage? I asked the driver and he has no idea. Now he's singing along to 'Blurred Lines' by Robin Thicke. We haven't gotten off on the best foot.

Anyway. Consider this my non-apology for ghosting out of your party just now. You don't know I'm gone yet, of course. You probably think I'm just getting a drink, or in the bathroom, or out the front having a drunken fight via text with my boyfriend. In thirty minutes, you'll slur something about me being gone for 'fuckin' ages' and stage an emergency search party, but you won't find me. By the point you realise I'm gone I'll either be blissfully sleeping or being rushed to the emergency room to have my stomach pumped for aforementioned reasons that I will not go back into at the risk of gagging or – even worse – vomiting all over the back seat of this man's Toyota Camry. I have a 4.5-star rating as it is, okay? I can't risk it.

You might think I'm rude for bailing on your party without so much as an air kiss. I understand that it's considered 'proper etiquette' to do the rounds and say goodbye to every person I have ever met before I depart.

But let's be real: ghosting is, without a doubt, the superior way to exit a soirée. Also, I just saw your cousin Elise licking the inside of a random dude's mouth while he massaged her boob, so to hell with etiquette.

Why am I so proud of my mid-party ghost, you ask?

Well, first of all, I don't have to incur any of that *'But it's only 12.30!'* guilt that inevitably arises whenever anyone tries to leave a party before 2 am. I don't need to concoct a lie that I have another mate's birthday to attend, or an obscure footy function to rush off to. Instead, I can just vanish without a trace – like a highly-skilled ninja, or Robin Thicke's singing career.

Secondly, you don't need to worry about whether me leaving at midnight means people are having a bad time. Let me tell you: I had a great time! The music? Ten out of ten. The speeches? Amazing. Your outfit? Love it. If we were twenty-one again, this is the kind of party I'd be at until the sun rises. But you know what? We're not twenty-one anymore. I have a family breakfast locked in for 10 am tomorrow and as much as I cherish our friendship, wine hangovers make me want to die now.

My point is: I didn't mean to be rude, or ungrateful, or impolite. I just wanted to get home and cocoon myself in a doona. Also, these heels are brand new. I honestly don't know how many times in my life I'm going to make the mistake of trying to break in new heels at a party. All I know is my big toes feel like they're going to fall off.

When it's my birthday, feel free to get the fuck out of there ASAP. Your cheek-kisses on the way out will do nothing but rub off my carefully applied $70 bronzer. So if anything, you ghosting me would be a lovely favour. I implore you to do the same thing.

Every woman for herself, I say. I will continue to be shameless in my pursuit of eight hours of sleep and healthy priorities. I apologise for nothing.

Yours in friendship, love, and eternal ghosting,

Me xxxx

The kinds of invisible labour young women carry

- Being asked 'How long do I microwave this for?' by a man nearby as he holds the packet of food, with the cooking instructions in his direct line of vision.

- Being tasked with the role of step-in psychological counsellor whenever your male friend goes through a break-up.

- Being tasked with the role of step-in psychological counsellor whenever your boyfriend goes through a work conflict, friendship disagreement or family drama, because he's never been taught to discuss anything beyond beers and footy with the boys, saving all of his emotional baggage solely for you.

- Being expected to manage the intensive household chores that require fortnightly upkeep: the toilet, the oven, the fridge and the mould on the bathroom ceiling.

- Thinking about what to cook for dinner. Every. Fucking. Night.

- Coming up with an alternative when your first option 'isn't healthy' or 'isn't what I feel like tonight'.

- Buying a birthday card for his brother, sister, mum, dad, uncle, grandpa, chihuahua.

- Organising the present he didn't even know he needed to buy.

- Wrapping the present he didn't even know he needed to buy.

- Gifting the present he didn't even know he needed to buy, at the birthday event he didn't know he needed to attend.

- Booking movie tickets. And dinner reservations. And doctor's appointments.

- Remembering the times of all of the above.

- Taking the pill at the same time every day, because of course contraception is your burden to bear.

- Having every single person in the office turn and point to you when they are faced with the most obvious and self-explanatory admin question.

- Brainstorming fun and, more importantly, affordable (!!!) ways to celebrate Andrea from HR's final day in the office.

- Making sure every single person in the office signs Andrea from HR's jumbo card in the boardroom before laser tag commences at 3 pm.

- Being relied upon to clear away all the half-filled wine glasses and stack the office dishwasher after Andrea has left the building.

- Being relied upon to unstack the office dishwasher at 9 am the following Monday.

- Feeling like a nag for daring to gently ask a man to do any of the above.

- Silently stewing over the invisible labour of having to think about all that fucking invisible labour.

A rough and tumble on...
women with opinions

On Mon, 26 Aug 2020 at 3:52 PM,
Michelle Andrews <michelleandrews@shameless.com> wrote:

>>> Goooood afternoon, Zara McDonald! Happy new email thread!

I want to talk to you about being a woman in the public eye and, more specifically, being a woman in the public eye *with opinions*. By virtue of us sharing (feminist) social commentary online, we know that not everyone will like us. In fact, some people on the glorious, terrifying, disgusting, enlightening, bewildering interwebz might actually ... you know ... kinda hate us.

The example that comes to my mind is when we became the unwitting targets of a football trio's larrikin rant in June 2019. We had only just returned from our mid-year break when we were sent their podcast episode by some of our listeners and, well, it turns out they *really didn't like* what we were doing. We had never met any of the three men, and we certainly hadn't mentioned any of them on our show, but it was pretty clear that upon finding our relationship podcast *Love Etc.* at the top of the Australian podcast charts, they decided our content was stupid and embarrassing, and had no problem saying so in between fits of raucous laughter. In fact, so offended were they by our work, they'd decided to play snippets of our podcast on their show, and pick them apart piece by piece.

I remember listening to their segment about us and thinking, *Wow, these three middle-aged men are so irritated by us and what we have to say.* I laughed it off, sure, but I also felt wounded and anxious. Here were three men, two of them in their forties, playing snippets of two twentysomething women and sniggering at our audacity in being honest about sex and dating. In some moments, they were laughing so much they struggled to speak.

I remember standing on the steps of my apartment building later that day and saying to you, 'These kinds of sexist attitudes are why we began our podcast in the first place. We have to do something about it.' You weren't too sure at first, but eventually you agreed.

Do you still agree now, knowing what unfolded in the weeks after?

On Mon, 26 Aug 2020 at 4:27 PM,
Zara McDonald <zaramcdonald@shameless.com> wrote:

>>> My short answer is yes, I think we did the right thing by saying something. Their conversation was steeped in sexism, and I am glad we drew attention to that, because I am still firmly of the belief that so many people don't know what sexism looks like today – often, it's far more subtle and pervasive than we think. Sexism looks like older men being condescending, and denigrating women for their interests. I think I said in the episode where we called them out that I am acutely aware that by virtue of our age, gender and subject matter, people think we are stupid. This was the first time I had seen it expressed so blatantly.

Some context, for those playing at home who have no idea what happened next: we took issue with their comments, so we unpacked them on our podcast. When we did, it drew more attention than we ever, ever anticipated. Our listeners were impassioned and outraged, and the story started to gain momentum. Their listeners came for us, ours for them, and it became a storm neither you nor I was ready for. Within days, their podcast lost its sponsors, recording studio and eventually fell apart altogether.

VOICE

I think it was the first time I understood the reality of being a woman who was public (and unashamed) in her opinions. People tell you to shut up, infer you're unruly, make the assumption that you're mouthy and almost uncontrollable. And even though the most logical part of me knew we did the right thing, I still felt *embarrassed*. Like we were at the centre of drama I wanted no part in, like everything would be easier if we just stayed quiet.

Did those thoughts ever enter your mind?

On Mon, 26 Aug 2020 at 5:54 PM,
Michelle Andrews <michelleandrews@shameless.com> wrote:

>>> I definitely knew the easier option would have been to say nothing. Every single day that I woke up and saw the news headlines (or, on one particularly bizarre day, an almost full-page newspaper story) I thought, *Wow, we really didn't take the easy option here, did we?* But I also knew, deeply, that what's easy isn't always what's best. We chose the difficult route, sure, but we also chose the right one.

This is the thing that irks me though, right? Our response to their segment was one of the most balanced and calm things we've ever produced. We knew the conversation would go nowhere if we stooped to their level, so to combat their mockery, we armed ourselves with critical thinking and humour. We also knew that calling a piece of content 'sexist' would open a can of aggrieved white guys insisting we need to 'take a joke, sweetheart'. And so, we followed all the rules that women are told to follow to be taken seriously. We were not shrill. We didn't throw names around. We didn't raise our voices. We didn't take things too seriously. We didn't take *ourselves* too seriously. We barely even mentioned their podcast name! We simply laid out all of the reasons why their segment on us was a little bit fucked up, and then we thanked them – and every man who has derided a woman for her interests – for being a key reason why *Shameless* is successful. And then we giggled about the absurdity of it all, because, well, *what the actual fuck?*

We returned their serve. That was it.

When I played our segment to my little sister Evelyn the night before it was published, she thought we didn't go in hard enough, that we could have been more forthright in our analysis. Many of our listeners thought the same. They were proud of us for saying something, but believed we were *too measured* in our reply to what were some pretty screwed-up taunts. Ultimately, there was no perfect way to handle a situation like that, but I'm proud of what we produced. I'm also proud of the fact that, in the weeks after, we didn't say another word publicly, whereas the other podcast shared streams of belligerent posts on their Instagram and Twitter accounts. While they kicked and screamed and poured petrol on the corpse of their show, we moved on. We had bigger and better things to channel our energy into.

When journalists started writing about the podcast 'feud', they stumbled upon another segment where the footy trio joked about sexual assault, a segment that no spin doctor or toxic-masculinity surgeon could save. It was the flaming match that lit their show on fire.

Did we bring them undone single-handedly? Absolutely not. That's the thing that irked me most: to some, you and I were to blame for these men losing their jobs. Forget the fact that they are fully grown men who giggled about rape, it was somehow our fault that they were jobless. I think that says a lot about how we treat women in the public eye. *Speak your mind, until you say something the people in power don't want to hear.*

Yes, we had rubbed a few fragile men the wrong way, and they let us know as such in vile emails, podcast reviews, DMs and comments (*you're a slut, you're a whore, you're a frigid virgin, you're out to destroy a man's life, you're a selfish bitch, you've got it coming for you*) but whenever my mind slipped into unhelpful thoughts about us having made a mistake, I managed to pull myself back. We didn't make a mistake at all, we stuck up for ourselves. We had our own backs and, as a chronic people-pleaser, having my own back hasn't always come naturally.

It was a pretty shitty couple of weeks, but when I look back on what you and I have done together, I'm really fucking proud of that time. We were brave.

It makes me wonder, though. We played by all the rules, yet some people were still hell-bent on depicting us as mouthy women who lacked a sense of humour. Why do you think that was? Did we do anything that you look back on and regret?

On Mon, 26 Aug 2020 at 6:33 PM,
Zara McDonald <zaramcdonald@shameless.com> wrote:

>>> The concept of the 'easy option' is interesting to me, because I've spent so much time looking back on the drama and genuinely wondered why any woman would throw herself, willingly, in the centre of something like this, given the intensity and the aggression of the backlash. Yes, I said I would go back and do it all again, but I still wince as I write that. It's not like I would run back into the fire with total self-assuredness. I'd run back in, but I'd be closing my eyes, riddled with doubt and overcome with fear.

When you ask why so many considered us mouthy, regardless of the fact we were stupidly calm in our response, I think my answer is both sad and simple. If you're a woman publicly pushing back on men who make gross and denigrating jokes, you will forever be seen as the one who needs to loosen up. It doesn't matter how measured or calm or reasonable you are; if you take offence at a joke, then you, as the woman, automatically become the problem. You are the barrier to fun, the antidote to banter, the person who cares too much.

I don't think we ever stood a chance. We were always going to cop it, because whichever way we wrapped it, we still had a contrary opinion. It may have been communicated patiently and delicately, but it was still an opinion. And, like we keep coming back to, a woman with a challenging opinion is an unruly woman.

That said, though, I take solace in the fact we were measured, because imagine how vicious the divide would have been if we weren't. Imagine, for a second, if we had communicated with emotion. I'm not sure we would have emerged so unscathed. If there's one thing the world hates more than a woman with opinions, it is a woman who is emotional about her opinions.

We've gone back and forth about how we reflect on that time, but say something similar happened again and we were forced to stand up for ourselves: how would you approach it? How would you mentally prepare? What would you change?

On Mon, 26 Aug 2020 at 7:15 PM,
Michelle Andrews <michelleandrews@shameless.com> wrote:

>>> I actually think I would approach it in the exact same way – with critical analysis and a splash of humour. I would absolutely change how I handled the fallout, though.

As much as I felt proud of us for standing up to those men, I also felt crippling anxiety whenever a new fury-spitting email interrupted my little brother's birthday dinner. On a couple of occasions, Mitch and my sisters had to sit with me and coax me back into thinking reasonably, into seeing things as they actually were, not how my catastrophising brain was extrapolating them to be.

So, what would I change next time?

I think I would need to prepare my family and friends for it more. I lean on the people around me in those moments of overwhelming stress, and it's probably not very pleasant for me to bombard their phones with 'SHIIIIIIIIT I'VE JUST WALKED HEADFIRST INTO A NEWS CONTROVERSY' messages on a Wednesday afternoon, or 'FUCK NOW IT'S IN THE NEWSPAPER' on a Saturday morning. I would need to gently inform them that they might be seeing my name in the news, and that I'm okay, but that I don't want to hear about any of the

VOICE

commentary online unless I specifically ask for a synopsis of it. I would apologise to them, too, because they're bound to get questions from their own friends and co-workers, and that's not always a pleasant or particularly fun position to be in.

As for me? I would turn my phone off sooner and go to the gym. There is nothing to be gained from checking my Instagram message requests in the middle of a storm. You can't reason with trolls on the internet, no matter how hard you may try. Really, all you can do is block, delete, and move on with your day as best you can. Don't read and re-read their messages. If a person thinks you 'resemble Voldemort', then you probably won't be able to persuade them otherwise in 280 characters or fewer. Also, I don't look like Voldemort. I just don't. Snape, maybe. But the Dark Lord? No. I have a nose, for starters.

I'm also glad that when (and I say 'when' because I'm sure there will be another public controversy down the track, because there will always be old men who take aim at the ideas, interests and bodies of young women) we do find ourselves in a similar position, we have something like this to read and remember.

We didn't let our spirits become infected with pettiness or immaturity. We healed. We kept walking. We busied ourselves with the very important happenings in Buckingham Palace and the *Bachelor* mansion. The eyes that were on us quickly found something new and interesting to focus their attention on.

What will you be telling yourself, the next time we find two bullseyes on our backs?

On Mon, 26 Aug 2020 at 8:03 PM,
Zara McDonald <zaramcdonald@shameless.com> wrote:

>>> I will tell myself three things.

The first is that no one cares about what you're doing as much as you think they do. It's easy to assume, when you feel swallowed by your own story, that people are paying as much attention as you are. They're not. Truthfully, no one actually cares that much and with that realisation comes incredible power and freedom. Drop the ego, stop caring what people think and say what you think instead. Being fearless doesn't have to come naturally, it can be learned. Fearlessness can come from the understanding that the world will not end if you come under fire for putting yourself out there, so push against the grain, swim upstream, jump off the bandwagon.

The second is that this too shall pass. Controversies blow over: they always have and they always will. No story outlives and outruns a weekly news cycle. This too will fall out of people's memories. That doesn't give you licence to keep quiet rather than speaking out when you believe in something; it's just to say that eventually the tornado will spin elsewhere, and havoc will find a new home.

The third thing I would say is that standing up for what you care about and being likeable may not always marry. Sometimes you need to pick a side. Assuming both can go hand in hand in a world that still resents and denigrates the women who speak up might set you up for inevitable disappointment. Manage your expectations, because you cannot be everything to everyone. The faster you realise that, the faster you'll pick a side and articulate your position next time.

So speak without fear or shame, because your voice matters mightily and the world is better for hearing it.

VOICE

The space between what I thought I'd do and what I did

— MICHELLE —

For a long time I really, truly believed I would never share this publicly.

It's been seven years, and over those seven years I have oscillated between being open and being private. Again and again, hundreds of times, I resolutely settled on the latter. The safer option. The one that doesn't scratch at old wounds and risk drawing blood. After all, there's being open, and then there's *being open*. Sharing my mental illness with the masses was one thing; telling thousands of people about the worst thing to ever happen to me is another entirely.

For a very long time, this story was something I shared carefully with only those closest to me. My sisters, Evelyn and Claire, who were told a softer, gentler version in our family's lounge room in March 2013. My high school best friends, who were told in the back seat of my car that April. My boyfriend Mitch, on our third date in 2016. My psychologist, at the beginning of our first-ever session in June 2017. Zara, over a Thai green chicken curry in June 2018.

For so long, I was great at keeping the story controlled and contained. Despite my reputation as the world's worst secret-keeper, this was a secret I wanted to entomb. Every passing month reignited an urgency to dig and dig and dig, ferociously and without reprieve, in the hope that maybe I could bury the pain. But, as my psychologist told me once, when you don't confront trauma, it will slowly seep into every aspect of your life. That's why therapists don't worry too much about the patients who are visibly distraught in the days after a cataclysmic event; they worry about the ones who have remained quiet and still. That person was me, until I learned that pain cannot be buried.

When you bury pain beneath your feet, all it does is grow.

I want you to know what happened to me in the second week of January 2013, when I was eighteen years old, but I also want to protect myself. In other iterations of this piece, I walked through my sexual assault in granular detail: where I was, what I was wearing, what happened, how it felt to have my power over my own body stripped away until I felt like I was nothing.

Part of me wanted you to know the details out of a desire to be believed. But over time I've come to realise that my healing isn't dependent on what you think. I know what happened. I was there. It happened to me.

The thought of handing over the gritty details to be read by anyone feels like a new loss of control, a fresh form of trauma. Giving the world that kind of power is too painful. And so, there won't be a titillating account of my sexual assault in these pages.

Instead, I'll tell you what you need to know.

You need to know that I was sexually assaulted at a small gathering by a friend of a friend. You need to know that while it was happening, I was consumed with embarrassment that I hadn't shaved. You need to know that he pinned me down by my shoulders, and his pressure left finger-shaped bruises across my arms and collarbones for the next week. You also need to know that the deepest cut was not the assault itself, it was sobbing so hard I thought I was going to choke. It was the immediately apparent fact that, compared to a drunk man, I was physically weak – totally and completely incapable of defending myself.

You need to know that once it was over, I pretended that nothing had happened. I was too terrified to scream, too exhausted to escape. I went to sleep next to him. I woke early, and as I stared at the sunlight glowing through the gaps in the curtains, an all-consuming dread slammed into me. I was lying beside him, completely naked, with no idea where he had put my clothes. Unless I wanted him to see my bare body in the daylight, I needed to patiently wait for him to retrieve my dress, my bra, my undies, from wherever he had stashed them.

You need to know that once I was clothed and reunited with my phone, I went to Hungry Jack's. I ate a medium chips and sipped on a Coke. I listened to my girlfriend tell me about her crush on a boy she had just met.

You need to know that once I got home, I sat in bed and stared at my wardrobe doors, and made a promise to myself to be conveni-ent, to be uncontroversial, and to dig,

and dig,

and dig.

Before That Night, I was always disappointed when I heard stories of victims of sexual assault not reporting their experiences. What if the man who did these awful things could be found guilty and punished? What if he could be brought to justice? What if another woman suffered as a result of their silence?

Only, when it happened to me, all the 'buts' shouted just as loudly. What if I'm overreacting? What if this ruins my life? What if it ruins his? What if this is just a really, really, really bad mistake – one he regrets with all his soul? What if my friends and family find out? What if I'm judged for being drunk, or wearing a dress, or being in a house with boys I don't know well? What if I'm made to retrace the worst night of my life over and over again, in a way that won't ever let me forget it? What if, after months of public scrutiny, I'm made out to be a fraud? What if the pain of telling my story outweighs the pain of being powerless?

More than anything, I wish I could tell you I didn't accept his friend request on Facebook. I wish I could tell you that I didn't become friends with the people there that night. I wish I could tell you that I didn't go out with them most weekends to bars and clubs and music festivals for the next twelve months. I wish I could tell you that I didn't laugh at his jokes, put my arm around his shoulder, make him feel like he did nothing wrong. I wish I could tell you that, for a time, my smiling face wasn't on his social media profiles. I wish I could tell you that eighteen-year-old Michelle was better than that; that she had more self-respect, that she was stronger, that she stood up for herself, that she didn't befriend a predator out of a petulant desire to be liked by the boys she met.

It kills me that I can't tell you any of those things.

I know you're probably wondering why. Why would I want to keep a man like this in my life after what he had done to me? It's a good question, one that I ask myself all the time.

I guess the best way to explain it is self-preservation. I was eighteen and didn't want to be the girl who was sexually assaulted at a house party. I did not want to be the girl who lost control. If I could minimise what happened in that bedroom to just a bad sexual experience, if I could smile politely when he and his friends rocked up to Saturday night pre-drinks, then life could continue as normal. If I told the truth, then my life before and after That Night would be cleaved into two very separate things. I would be brandished with a scarlet 'A' for attention seeker, a 'V' for victim, 'L' for liar. I would open up the floodgates of incredulity and disbelief, because the first lesson of Sexual Assault 101 is the woman will be considered a conniving opportunist until she proves otherwise.

Before That Night, I was too busy doing BuzzFeed quizzes to find out which kind of cheese I am to ever really concern myself with feminist literature or intelligent analysis of rape culture. My understanding of both paled in comparison to what I know now. My assault didn't feel legitimate because it didn't mirror what I had seen in movies or read about in books. My rapist wasn't a knife-wielding monster, lurking in a shadowy alleyway. He was a teenager who wore too much gel in his hair. He was a friend of a friend. He was . . . familiar.

I can only imagine the look on your face, reader, if I showed you a photograph of him. I think your eyes would widen. Your mouth would gape, just a little. You'd look up at me and ask, 'Really? This guy?' And I'd say yes, this guy. The guy who seems totally and completely ordinary. Friendly. A little shy, even.

Scary, isn't it? We always think of the one in five women who claim they have been sexually assaulted – who they are, what they look like – but rarely consider that the men perpetrating those assaults could very well be our brothers, co-workers, friends. The inconvenient truth is that the average rapist is not a breathy weirdo, waiting to snatch you on a cold winter's night. The average rapist walks amongst us, claiming the women in his direct orbit as prey. He probably watches the same TV shows you do. Spends his weekend mornings at brunch like you do. Wastes too much time on Instagram like you do.

It took a lot of time to unstitch and reweave the narrative of That Night because it didn't match anything I had been told about rape and rapists. Perhaps that's why the language I used to tell the story to family and friends changed as time went on, and I had the opportunity for my head to catch up with my body. When I explained That Night to my sisters, the first people I ever told, I said 'he took advantage of me'. When I told my girlfriends a month later, I said 'he forced himself on me'. When I told Zara at twenty-four, I said 'he sexually assaulted me'.

Forget leaving that house party and visiting the local police station to file a report. It took months for me to even tell the true story to myself. By then the bruises had long faded, the traces of him were gone. All that remained was the shell of my being.

One that was cracking.

Something odd happens when bad men touch you.

The terrible man's hands and mind are what's foreign and hideous, of course, but somehow coming into contact with them makes you those things, too. The ugliness of the exchange is passed on like a disease.

When I was sixteen, I was positively giddy to be invited to a popular boy's birthday party. I wore a black singlet from Supré and a floral skirt my sister had made in mat-tech (short for 'materials technology', also short for 'hell on earth') because I couldn't afford to buy anything else. I blinked mascara onto my eyelashes and painted my nails pink. I shaved my legs with a razor that I found stuck inside a special edition of *Cosmopolitan*. I felt pretty. Grown-up.

I poured vodka into my soft drink and winced at the taste. I flirted with a boy whose hair flopped over his eyes, giggling inanely at every word that exited his lips. I took my first ever drag from a cigarette and stifled a cough when the smoke hit my throat. I looked at my face in the bathroom mirror, enchanted by the sweet warmth of drunkenness. The centre of my lips was bright, raspberry red. My eyes were bloodshot.

When the party was over, I went out to the street to call a taxi home. My girlfriends and I were standing in a circle chatting to some of the boys we'd just met when I felt a hand reach up my skirt. I froze as if a current of electricity had just zapped my body. A person was behind me, and their hand was touching my underwear. A boy had never touched me there before, and now a boy was touching me there in front of a group of people. His fingers were sliding across the fabric of my undies in search for flesh – flesh he wouldn't find. Why? Because between those undies and my flesh was another layer that he hadn't accounted for: my period pad.

His hand recoiled at the realisation and I was overcome with disgust. Sure, the guy was a creep – I later found out he'd spent half the night putting his hands up girls' skirts – but it wasn't just that. I felt disgusting, too. I was the girl wearing the pad. I was the girl who looked pretty in her flowery skirt until he realised what it was concealing.

I was a disappointment, somehow. A girl who had seemed desirable until this boy got up close, saw her for what she really was, and realised she wasn't what he wanted at all.

I was the girl who wasn't ready to be used.

It took a few years of trying to bury That Night in January 2013 for my mental health to unravel.

In 2014, I cut off contact with almost every person who slept in that house because I couldn't bear to be near him anymore.

I began listening to true-crime podcasts with voracious interest, as if learning the details of other violent sexual assaults would educate me, and insulate me from ever being in the same position again. I pored over the profiles of murderers and rapists, looking for threads of behaviour and warning signs. I flinched with fear whenever a strange man brushed past me in public, particularly on the tram on my way to work. I saw danger everywhere. I saw it in every man I met.

I tried desperately to move on, to write that night off as an awful experience, but one I wouldn't let define me. Only, my assault was bleeding into my dreams, morphing them into nightmares that jolted me awake while our beachside town slept. I became an incessant sleep-talker, a person who was haunted at night. As much as I tried to deny it during the day, nightfall revealed the truth: my demons weren't just sticking their fingernails out of the soil I had covered them in, they were ricocheting off my heart and careening down my throat, dancing on my soul and coming to life when I shut my eyes.

By the time I walked into my psychologist's waiting room in 2017, I felt emotionally bankrupt. I went into the first appointment thinking my anxiety was the culmination of a few things – my parents' separation, my acute glandular fever, the unreasonable demands of my job – but really, all I wanted to speak about was That Night. With a box of tissues in hand, I told my psychologist everything. I told her that I felt like I was going to explode, that I would do anything to escape my body, that I could scream and scream and scream and scream and scream and scream for ever letting him into my life.

My psychologist asked me to do two things. The first: write him a letter, and the second: get a gym membership.

The letter wasn't one that I would ever send; it was to help me map out the contours of my wound and devise a plan to treat it.

In it, I told him how he made me sick. How I pitied him. How small and insignificant he had made me feel. How he was a coward, but so was I. Then I told him about how successful I was going to be. How I was going to prove that he didn't have control over me anymore. That I had every intention of recovering and living a brilliant life free from fear, free from him.

My psychologist's reasoning behind the gym membership was simple: she wanted me to feel stronger, mentally and physically. The push to start treating my body with the respect it deserves is one of the greatest gifts anyone has ever given me.

After our second session, in which my psychologist read my letter while I stared at the trees outside her office, I burnt it in my sink. I watched the flames engulf the pages and decided, *Enough.*

I have only seen him once, at a music festival, since I stopped hanging out with that group in 2014. I pointed him out to my boyfriend, Mitch, with shaky hands and glassy eyes, whispering in his ear who that guy in the T-shirt was. Since then, we haven't crossed paths. Actually, while I think of what happened to me all the time, I don't think of him much at all. When I told Zara the story of that night over dinner in the Thai restaurant, it took me a few minutes to remember his surname.

Even so, I still replay what happened in my head every single week. I have flipped it back and forth. I have revisited it when I am sober and when I am drunk. I have tried to write about it, have spoken about it, dreamed about it. I have re-examined it so many times that it truly feels like it happened to another woman.

Would I respond differently if it happened to me today? Absolutely. If this happened to me at twenty-six, I know I would do something, go to the police. I would tell someone – anyone – before it was too late. But I lacked the life experience and the gumption to know with unwavering conviction that I had been abused. I was a teenager, a girl whose parents still did her laundry and made her dinner every night.

I never planned on telling my story. The weakest part of myself still wants to delete this essay, to not include it in the pages that you're reading. But in the years since, I have learned that other girlfriends have had similar experiences. They have also remained silent in the aftermath of their sexual assault, only for the fury to ignite a blaze in their body and torch their sense of self until it becomes ash. I have spoken to so many others who feel the guilt of staying silent, of not reporting, of taking out a shovel when they wish they took out an axe.

I have witnessed the desolation of too many women. Women whose teens and twenties have been marred by untold stories that will never be accounted for in police records or statistics. Women who watch sexual assault trials play out in the media and feel a concoction of sympathy, relief and despair, knowing that they'll never be pillaged of their humanity, but they'll never see justice carried out either. If you're one of these women, I want you to know that it's okay. That your silence doesn't eliminate what happened to you. That we didn't ask for any of this. And that it's not our fault.

I also want you to know that now, as I write this, I am happy – happier than I've ever been.

It took time for me to get here. Years of therapy and lifting weights and running until my legs gave out. But all those tears I cried? They nourished that soil at my feet. They turned the wasteland of my being into an emerald-green forest, brimming with life, energy, newness. I vanquished the demons and found angels in their place – a wonderful partner, a glorious family, and magical friends who embolden me with their support. I have a career that I adore, hobbies that enrich me, a *Love Island* addiction that's showing no sign of decay.

I am alive. I am fulfilled. I am free.

And, reader, I am so much more than okay.

So here we are. Seven years on.

Sharing this with you is not easy, and I'm scared – bloody terrified, actually – but I know I'm ready. Why? Because it's the helpful thing to do.

The guilt I feel over not reporting what happened is still there, a gentle hum in the background of my life. I didn't do what I thought I would, and that's something I am still coming to terms with. I did what I could in a situation that I wouldn't wish on anyone. I did what I could to protect what was left of my eighteen-year-old self. I did what the vast majority of women do, because the world we live in gives us very little choice.

This story will always be a part of who I am. This experience of feeling powerless, voiceless, meaningless, has been baked into much of what I do. It's why the goal of making women feel heard – making them feel seen in a world that sometimes looks the other way – is one I care so deeply about. It's why I bought my own microphone and started to speak into it. It's why I strive to be noisy and utterly fucking shameless about the stuff that matters to me.

A man tried to squash me that night, but he didn't win.

Because look at me now.

The space beyond

We were terrified to leave our jobs at Mamamia with no real plan of what was going to happen next. We had minds full of doubt, with a sea of one million unanswered questions stretching before our feet. We had our guts, nudging us to the edge of the cliff. We had a circle of supportive family and friends, screaming at us to just jump already. And we had our friendship, gently reassuring us that it's not that far when things felt particularly scary and overwhelming.

We didn't know if we could swim. We've learned in the two years since that you'll never know until you try. All you can do is fall through the air, close your eyes, and trust you'll overcome whatever happens when your body slips into the water.

We plunged off the cliff and into the sea and we've been finding our way ever since.

Your twenties can be hard. (Hell, we've still got a few years to go and we know that to be true.) Making decisions blind can be even harder. But if we've learned anything it's that there was perhaps no other time in our lives where we could have made the leap.

In the space between the land and water, we found our way to a job we love and a community of powerful women who challenge us to be better every day. Most importantly, well, we found each other.

The space is scary but it's also really bloody lovely, too. It has showed us a lot more about who we are, what we want and the

THE SPACE BEYOND

people we intend to be. There will be more of these uncharted spaces as we continue through life – multitudes of them, in fact. Spaces between fear and ambition, love and loss, loneliness and chaos. These years were always going to be scary, and we won't always have the answers.

But when we commit to moving through the doubt anyway? That's where the growth is.

Acknowledgements

There are so many people we want to thank for making these pages come to life – about 387, actually. We won't be able to thank every single one of you, though, because if this were the Oscars, Penguin Random House would be playing their 'get off the stage' music already.

So, here are our top forty-two.

To Izzy Yates, whose steady hand moulded this book into something we are really proud of. Thank you for seeing something in us so, so long ago and for taking such a crazy chance on two numbnuts who know very little about the world. We are indebted to you and your brilliant, clever, insightful editing. We are smarter for having worked under you.

Our copyeditor, Genevieve Buzo, whipped these words into shape. Your editing suggestions occasionally spiralled us into existential crises but you've ultimately made us better writers who will be more sparing with the word 'currency' in the future. (Please don't edit this acknowledgement.)

Monique Bowley was the first person who heard our obnoxious twitterings and demand we be put in a studio together. She was also the first person who ever said yes to us in Podcast Land, and for that we will always be so thankful. (Also! Instructing us to not sign with a podcast network and stay working for ourselves was the best career advice we have ever been given.)

To our stupidly intelligent friends Sophie Aubrey and Brittany Stewart, thank you for sitting through countless dinners in which we vented and rambled and moaned. You are two of the kindest, most generous people we know and so many of the stories in this book are infused with your friendship.

To Genevieve Day: thank you for being a pivotal person in our careers. We are so grateful for you finding us as early as you did, and will always cherish the time we spent as a little team.

Annabelle Lee is one of our favourite people. She has this strange habit of dancing when she feels awkward. Thank you for being our jack-of-all-trades, and for never complaining when we force you to tell us about your love life/social outings/personal life when we all really should be working.

To Zoë Foster Blake, Jamila Rizvi and Sam Cavanagh: thank you for offering invaluable writing and podcasting advice whenever we come knocking. None of you boast publicly about how much you do to help young people in this industry, and we really wish you did. The world needs more people like you.

To the writers who may have no idea who we are, but have incredible influence over the way we think (Jia Tolentino, Carly Findlay, Hadley Freeman, Sally Rooney, Taffy Brodesser-Akner, Dolly Alderton, Pandora Sykes, Kiley Reid, Clementine Ford, Caity Weaver, Roxane Gay): thank you for making us smarter, just by virtue of putting work into the world.

To every 'In Conversation' guest who said 'yes' to coming on the podcast and giving us their time, particularly in the early days, when we were tiny and irrelevant: thank you. You didn't need to do anything for us, and we are eternally grateful that you did.

And of course to you, our community. You make us smarter, more thoughtful people, who spend far too much time debating the merits and downfalls of wearing a dress with pockets. You feel like our real-life penpals and it is a privilege to be able to write and talk to you every day.

FROM ZARA

To my fierce friendship circle, with special mention to Emily, Sammy and Sakshi: thank you for always having my back. Without your understanding when I got a little bit too stressed, or went a little too M.I.A., these words would never have come. Also, to every single friend I cancelled dinner with because I had to 'write some more stuff', or 'edit some more words', thank you, thank you, *thank you* for being so kind about it.

My three siblings Joel, Mietta and Liam (and yes, Lachy, you too) are undoubtedly four of the best people I know. I will forever appreciate their ability to inflate my ego when my weird job gets me down, and deflate it when they think I take myself too seriously (which is like, always).

My parents, David and Trish, gave me the unique privilege of being able to chase any dream I ever had because I know at the end of it all, they will be right there waiting with cups of green tea and mini bars of Crunchie. I love you both heaps.

To Oli, the one who absorbs more of my stress and silliness than anyone, none of this has any meaning without you laughing from the sidelines. You are my safe space. Thank you for refusing to let my many crises of confidence tilt me sideways.

And of course, to Michelle: I should tell you more often how central you are to everything. Thank you for consistently keeping me afloat and for always politely telling me when I am wrong. You have a bigger heart and a better brain than me and I know there is no one else I could ever, ever, ever do this beside.

FROM MICH

Thank you to my parents Paul and Vicky, who taught me why eating dinner together at the dining table is so important. On top of unwavering love and support, you gave me the tools and the permission to find my voice. I'm sorry I sometimes use it for all that swearing.

My siblings Claire, Evelyn and Tom put up with me being the sick, wheezy kid for about twelve years and for that, they deserve a medal. A second, complimentary medal, too, for all the times I thrust a blog post in their faces and begged them to 'PLEASE JUST PROOFREAD THIS FOR A SECOND'.

Carolyn, you are the fifth sibling – never forget that. Who else would send me rogue 'Quick and Dirty' story suggestions about nuns and Akon's cryptocurrency, Akoin?

Nanny, you showed me the beauty of writing. This book is no Charles Dickens novel, but I hope you enjoyed reading it as much as I enjoy your work.

Mitchell, I love you. One day, sooner than you think (i.e. before we get that Golden Retriever), you'll tell me the Tigers are your second-favourite footy team. Until then, know that I consider myself so incredibly lucky to wake up next to you.

My schoolfriends Ayesha, Emily and Maddie kept my sanity intact in the early days of writing this book. Thank you for each showing me that there's no shame in binge-watching *Keeping Up with the Kardashians* and eating your body weight in Criniti's pizza. I'll respond to the group chat in a sec, I promise.

And finally, to my wonderful friend Zara: I couldn't do this with anyone but you, you absolute gem of a human. Thanks for not batting an eyelid when I ask if I can spend $208 on bespoke Michael Bublé posters. I'll buy you some salmon and rice with an apple kombucha to make up for it.